Romans and Christians AD 64

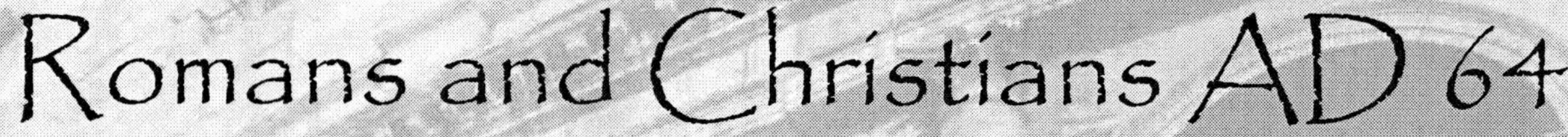

Romans and Christians AD 64

An Intergenerational Catechetical Experience of Martyrdom and Persecution in the Early Church

Andrea Lorenzo Molinari

WIPF & STOCK · Eugene, Oregon

ROMANS AND CHRISTIANS AD 64
An Intergenerational Catechetical Experience of Martyrdom and Persecution in the Early Church

Wipf and Stock Publishers
199 W. 8th Ave., Suite 3
Eugene, OR 97401

ISBN 13: 978-1-55635-845-6

Manufactured in the U.S.A.

I DEDICATE THIS BOOK TO my son, Roberto Xavier Molinari. Roberto, you have always served well, upholding your *sacramentum*, as a loyal "soldier" of the Emperor, my prayer for you is that you may learn to say with St. Maximilian:

> I will not accept the seal of this world; and, if you give it to me, I shall break it, for it is worthless. I am a Christian. I cannot wear a piece of lead around my neck after I have received the saving sign of Jesus Christ my Lord, the son of the living God. You do not know him; yet he suffered for our salvation; God delivered him up for our sins. He is the one whom all we Christians serve: we follow him as the prince of life and the author of salvation. (*Acts of Maximilian,* 6)

There are several people who deserve to be recognized as important contributors to this venture.

First, I wish to honor Christopher D. Alfaro and Jason R. Jeske who both helped me develop this project. They were present as advisors and collaborators from the earliest days as I began to create *Romans and Christians AD 64*. You were the very first to play the roles of Peter and Paul. No one has done it better.

Second, I want to express my appreciation to Bill Richer. He was a tremendous support as I worked to bring this project to publication. Our conversations and his suggestions have strongly influenced the final product. Your friendship and brotherhood is very precious to me.

Third, I owe a debt of gratitude to my dear friends Mitch and Julie Erickson. Their emotional and financial support of this project was absolutely essential. The DVD of the Rules that was created for this project simply would not exist without them. Their unassuming love is an ongoing witness to God's presence in my life.

Lastly, I wish to thank my sister, Noelle A. Molinari-McCormick, Ph.D., and my student and friend, Leonardo Pastore. Their assistance in traveling around Italy, helping me collect the photographs included in this volume added greatly to the final product. I owe you both "una birra fredda!"

. . . Remember me, and remember the faith. These things should not disturb you but rather strengthen you.

—the martyr, Saturus
in the *Martyrdom of Perpetua and Felicitas 10.4*

About the DVD . . .

Throughout this book reference is made to a DVD that has been created for *Romans and Christians AD 64*. The DVD is a *very* valuable resource intended to aide users of this game as they present it to both youth ministry core teams and, eventually, participants on the night of the event itself. The DVD is a video rulebook designed to explain the game in a clear and systematic fashion. It was created in order to lift the burden of explaining the game from the youth leader's shoulders, thus helping to ensure a smoother game experience for all.

The original publishing plan called for this DVD to be included along with this book. However, as the logistics of this plan were considered, it seemed more practical to direct the customer directly to the author for this component of the product.

Therefore please contact Andrea Lorenzo Molinari, Ph.D. at the following email address: andrealmolinari@netscape.net. If, for any reason, this email address ceases to be active in the future, access to the author and the DVD can be gained by contacting Wipf and Stock Publishers and requesting the most up-to-date email address for Dr. Molinari. The price of this DVD is $20.00 which is intended to cover production, shipping, and handling costs.

Future plans also include launching a website to provide further support for customers. When this website is launched, it should be found easily enough by searching under *Romans and Christians AD 64*.

Contents

Foreword

A Scholar's Viewpoint

WHEN ASKED WHY I became a professional student and teacher of early Christian origins, I always say that it is because I want to know *what it was like to be a Christian* in the earliest Church. Not chiefly out of an interest in pure history, nor even because I am personally committed to the great theological truths of the Bible and Christian doctrine, wonderful as these may be. No, it is the *experiential* dimension that I find most deeply fascinating: real men, women, and children, in many respects like me, who chose to follow Christ *in that world, back then.* I want to share their lives, even if most of the time it can only be by way of small glimpses, or partial moments—in fragments.

I wish now that, when I was a teenager going through Confirmation classes, our catechist had had access to something like Andrea Lorenzo Molinari's *Romans and Christians AD 64.* Because Molinari's role-playing game offers that experiential dimension to Christian education and formation, and it does so with remarkable power and grace. Grounded in more than twenty years of scholarly inquiry and college-level teaching, and adorned with numerous photographs, diagrams, and other illustrations, *Romans and Christians AD 64* is designed to bring such figures as Peter, Paul, and Nero to life; and not only these major voices, but also many lesser persons who made up the fabric of the Roman capital in which the Good News was preached "back then."

At the heart of the "game"—and the specter of those fearful Roman gladiatorial "games" is never far from sight—is each participant taking on a first-century identity, whether actual (Peter, Simon Magus, Prisca, et al.) or typical (a Roman soldier, slave, executioner). This includes the game's leaders and the participants' parents; hence "Intergenerational" in the game's subtitle. In a strategy reminiscent of the Jewish Holocaust Museum in Washington, D.C., where on entry visitors are invited to take the "identity card" of an actual victim, Molinari supplies the group of game-players with literally dozens of "character cards" to choose from. These cover the range of possible points of view, from high to low, from soldiers to strong believers to doubters to those who would rather not get caught up in controversy at all. For those especially engaged, there are straightforward instructions for making costumes and various other props, many out of standard household items.

Catechists and youth teachers will be reassured by repeated references, in the discussion of the Rules early on, to Molinari's extensive personal experience as a leader of the game: what seems to work well, or not so well; how to adapt to unusual situations. Molinari also suggests ways in which different church or school spaces might be adapted so that the action can include real movement from one game location (say, the Christians' meeting-place, or the jail) to another (say, a Roman *praetorium,* or the arena). The question, "Who can play which role?" is handled with characteristic common sense: in this "game" environment, there is no reason for a young woman not to assume the identity of an early Christian minister, or, for that matter, of Peter or Paul! And the progress of the game is set out with such direction and clarity as to convince the well-prepared leader that this 3 1/2-hour, multi-dimensional game—and, dare I say, *adventure*?—really can work very well.

Most impressive to me is the way that *Romans and Christians AD 64* relates such *practical* first- and later- century questions as the safety of the scriptures, the succession of Christian teachers and preachers, and the preservation of the martyrs' memory to the *religious* practice and emerging *theological* language of the early Church. From within that Church we come to see such familiar sequences as "out of error into truth, out of sin into righteousness, out of death into life" as having social and spatial dimensions in the opposing worlds of pagan Rome, on the one hand, and the community gathered in the name of its crucified and risen Lord, on the other.

As the text reminds us, the days of persecution are not over for many thousands of Christian men and women today. *Romans and Christians AD 64* shows us something of the historical starting-point, not, to be sure, of all persecution everywhere (we are also reminded of the Maccabees, for example), but of organized persecution and especially of martyrdom *in Jesus' name*. Today's catechumen will doubtless learn of his or her baptism as "dying and rising with Christ." Those who participate in *Romans and Christians AD 64* will come to appreciate more than most just how real and how close was the prospect of death to their earliest counterparts. They will also, I trust, savor all the more the Good News of eternal life proclaimed and bravely embraced by Christian men and women "back then."

—Julian V. Hills
Department of Theology
Marquette University

Foreword

A Youth Ministry Perspective

"Be doers of the word and not hearers only." (James 1:22)

THESE ARE SOME OF the first words that I recall Andrea Molinari speaking to me as I sat in a bible study at the Franciscan University of Steubenville. He knew how to bring the Scriptures to life. That freshman theology student I met all those years ago was filled with an enthusiasm and conviction that forever left an imprint on my soul. His passion for the Sacred Scriptures and his desire to bring them to life is still evident in the making of *Romans and Christians AD 64.*

We live in a technical age where our young people are raised sitting before a television fighting battles of good versus evil through the medium of video games. They are caught up in a world of fantasy and superheroes. They engage in battle after battle, each time trying to defeat the "enemy" so as to win the game. They are able to do this using three, four, or five lives, each time learning a new technique so that they can advance to the next level. In reality, we have only one "life." Perhaps the question is: what will we do with it?

The martyrs of the early Church fought more a heroic battle than our youth could ever comprehend. Yet, their battle was not a game. The early Christians knew that in order to follow Christ they may have to make the ultimate sacrifice. *Romans and Christians AD 64* brings this reality to life and gives youth and adults the chance to experience, at least in a small way, what being a hero really means.

—Christopher D. Alfaro
St. Thomas the Apostle Catholic Church
Grand Rapids, Michigan

Quo vadis? "Where are you going?" Not only is this the theme of what I believe to be one of the greatest games that has been created for youth ministry but it is also a question that I would ask (if I had the chance) any youth minister, who is serious about building their youth ministry programs and keeping students actively involved in their parish.

My name is Deacon Bill Richer. I have been a full time youth minister for over ten years at two different parishes in the Diocese of Des Moines, Iowa. Over nine years ago, Andrea Molinari, who I consider a personal friend, introduced me to *Romans and Christians AD 64*. As a youth minister I have planned, directed, and facilitated the game seven times. At my first parish, we began with 42 students participating. The next year it grew to 74. Three years later, the final time at my first parish assignment, we had 132 students involved. I can vividly remember having a discussion with Andrea the day after the game, with both of us agreeing: "This is it. This is the max. It can't and shouldn't get any bigger then this." Well, at my present position at St. Francis, the first year we had 96 students play the game. Now get ready for this: Last winter, exactly one year later, 204 students and over 45 adult volunteers played. Together we enjoyed a full evening that I would describe as the most awesome "whole family catechesis" game night for youth ministry I have ever experienced. The best part was the rave reviews from all involved. Need I say more?

So, where *are* you going? Where is your youth ministry program heading? Are you looking for a new educational, inspiring, role playing game that can be the talk of your students for days after they participate? This game is appropriate for middle school, high school, or both together. Are you looking for a game that not only will attract increased numbers, but will provide the opportunity to bring in full participation from parish staff, students, and most of all, parents? This is it! Less then two months ago, I did a survey on youth ministry for our high school students and asked them to list from 1–10 in order their favorite youth ministry events that we have offered. On every survey, *Romans and Christians AD 64* was listed as number 1 or 2. I believe that says it all.

Caution: This game *does* take planning. It *does* take time to put together. It is work. But with the help of the instructional DVD, anyone can do it. Anyone can pull it off, regardless of your experience, or the size of your parish. All you have to do is follow the simple instructions. Then get ready for all your young people coming to you asking, "When are we going to do it again?" It is an absolute can't miss hit for any youth ministry program. I'll stake my name on it. In fact I will put my email address on it. If you have any questions, please contact me: bricher@saintfrancischurch.org. May the blessings of God be upon all of you.

Christ's peace always,

—Deacon Bill Richer
Director of Youth Ministry
St. Francis Parish, West Des Moines, Iowa

Preface

Romans and Christians AD 64 is a role-playing game that is born out of both history and legend. On the one hand, it is set in Rome during the infamous Neronic Persecution of the mid to late 60s in the first century of our era. This bloody persecution is historical fact. On the other hand, many of the characters that appear in the game are taken directly out of the apocryphal legends associated with the ministries and deaths of Peter and Paul, known to us as the apocryphal acts of the apostles. Before proceeding, it is worth saying a few words about apocryphal literature in general and apocryphal acts of the apostles in particular.

Originally, the word "apocryphal" came from the Greek word ἀποκρύπτω or *apokrypto* which means "to keep hidden from or to hide from." This reflects an idea that was expressed in some examples of this early Christian literature, namely that these texts contained divinely revealed truths that had been revealed to an apostle or another historically significant holy person (e.g., Isaiah or Enoch) but then kept secret from the outside world. Later, as the Church began to form authoritative doctrines through the various Church

Figure 1

Figure 2

FIGURE 3

FIGURE 4

FIGURE 5

FIGURE 6

FIGURE 7

Figure 8a

Figure 8b

(continued from page xi)

councils such as Nicaea (325), the term apocryphal was applied to writings that were rejected by the Church as spurious and sometimes as heretical. Today, when applied to early Christian writings, the term "apocryphal" has the conventional sense of "extra-canonical." Because of this specter of the old meaning, when people (especially the more conservative) hear the word "apocryphal" they assume a defensive stance.

Figure 9

Never was this made clearer to me than when, during my tenure in Des Moines, I was confronted by a deacon after an adult education class in which I discussed several apocryphal texts. I was amused when this deacon told me quite sternly that he rejected all things apocryphal and could not begin to fathom why I might even consider teaching about apocryphal literature in my early Church history classes. I knew that this fellow was very traditional but that he was generally a nice person so I bit my tongue. I swallowed my pride and merely asked him if he would give me a fair chance to articulate my position on the matter. He conceded and I began by asking him a series of questions. First, I asked him, "How did Peter die?" He answered, "He was crucified upside-down." Second, I asked, "Well then, how did Paul die?" He replied, "He was beheaded." Pleased at his ready answers, I made one more query, "What were the names of the mother and father of Mary, the mother of Jesus?" The deacon beamed, being a traditional Catholic with a strong devotion to the Blessed Mother, proud that he was able to answer my question. "Their names were Anna and Joachim," he said. I sprang my trap. "Do you realize," I told him that every one of those "facts" that

Figure 10

you take for granted are parts of legends that come down to us through apocryphal texts? The story of Peter's martyrdom comes from the *Acts of Peter*. Likewise, the story of Paul's martyrdom comes from the *Acts of Paul*. Last but not least, the names of Mary's parents come to us from the *Protoevangelium of James*.

I would like to say that I won my debate partner over but the truth is that he stubbornly refused to accept what I was saying.

Many Christians are aware of the "facts" of the martyrdoms of Peter and Paul as well as the names of Mary's parents. Yet they have no idea where to find the associated stories. The truth is that the legends recounted in apocryphal literature are more a part of we will examine in greater detail below (as recorded in the *Acts of Peter* 32) (**see Figures 1–4**). Quite frankly, this is hardly unique as regards the artistic depiction of apocryphal stories involving Peter and Paul. One needs only to pass through the 15th century

Figure 11

Figure 12

Christian life and worship than most people would ever believe. This is especially true for Roman Catholics. For example, if one travels to Rome, in particular the Vatican City, and tours the Basilica of St. Peter, one must pass through the Atrium or porch of the famous basilica. The Atrium has a high, vaulted ceiling that is decorated with many octagonal carvings that are traced in golden trim. These carvings depict various scenes from the life of Peter ranging from stories narrated in the Gospels to those known only in apocryphal literature; including his battle with Simon Magus and the *Domine, quo vadis* story, which bronze doors that usher the visitor into the Basilica of St. Peter to be struck with highly detailed depictions of the martyrdoms of Peter and Paul (**see Figures 5–8**).

Inside the Basilica proper the visitor will find yet another piece of art that commemorates a story found only in an apocryphal source. I speak here of the altar dedicated to Saints Processo and Martiniano (**see Figure 9 and 10**). The altar honors two Roman guards who, according to the apocryphal work *Martyrdom of Peter* (a.k.a. Psuedo-Linus), were converted and baptized by Peter while he was incarcerated in the

Mammertine Prison in Rome. The Cappella di San Francesco Borgia in the Jesuit Church of the Gesù also boasts a painting of the baptism of of these two saints by Pier Francesco Mola. Related to this, if one visits the Mammertine Prison itself, one will be greeted with a marble plaque that lists the martyrs housed in the prison. The first line in the list reads *Pietro e Paolo Principi degli apostoli s Nerone Imp* (Peter and Paul,

Figure 13

Princes of the Apostles under Emperor Nero). The second reads, *Processo e Martiniano loro carcerieri s Nerone Imp* (Processus and Martinianus, their jailers, under Emperor Nero) (**see Figure 11**). Passing through the entrance into the prison, one descends a small stone staircase into the holding cell proper and sees an altar with a bronze relief that depicts the saints' baptism by the apostles (**see Figures 12–14**).

If one is interested in depictions of the crucifixion of St. Peter, in my opinion, one need not begin anywhere else but the Cerasi Chapel in Santa Maria del Popolo. There one will find the work of Carvaggio (**see Figure 15**). Certainly, more examples could be given, such as the moving painting of the crucifixion of St. Peter that is on display in the *Domine, quo vadis*? Chapel, located not far outside of Rome on the Via Appia (**see Figure 16**). However, the point here is that the legends that come down to us through the many apocryphal sources are part of the historical fabric of Christian art and worship and have clearly shaped the Christian imagination.

With these basic thoughts on apocryphal literature and its place in Church history in general, we can turn to a brief consideration of the apocryphal acts of the apostles in particular. The apocryphal acts of the apostles are legendary stories that were told in

Figure 14

the early churches reconstructing the continuing adventures of the apostles. The earliest of these texts is the *Acts of Paul*, which was likely written in the latter part of the second century and has its earliest attestation in the treatise, *On Baptism* (ca. 205) by the North African theologian, Tertullian. It is supposed that the *Acts of Peter* was also written in this same period. During the third, fourth, and fifth centuries many other legends were written in which apostles such as Andrew, Thomas, John, Philip, Matthias and others were presented as heroically advancing the cause of Christ.

Generally speaking, modern scholars believe that these stories were created with multiple purposes in mind. Certainly, these stories have a propagandistic function. They promote various theological positions (e.g., sexual asceticism, forgiveness of serious sin after baptism, etc.), essentially using the apostles Peter, Andrew, Paul, John and Thomas (among others) as advocates of these agendas. These apostles give homilies and speeches that campaign for their author's pet cause.

However, the apocryphal acts also have (and still have) a very palpable *entertainment* function. Simply put: they are just fun to read. Among the stories found in these charming texts Peter makes a salted-fish swim again and enters into a "raising the dead" contest with Simon Magus. Philip fights a dragon. Thomas gets sold as a slave by Jesus himself. Andrew preaches a long sermon from his cross and then dies on cue so as to defeat his enemy. Paul appears to Roman soldiers after

Figure 15

his execution. John, in a very Dr. Dolittle-esque way, talks to bed bugs! What could be better? It can be said that these acts have a populist appeal, presenting their themes not in high and unapproachable theology but in terms easily understood by common people.

In a very real sense we can say that these acts tell us much more about the theological tastes and sensibilities of the early centuries of the Church then they do about the life and times of the apostles and their associates. It should be stated here that many of these themes will be offensive to modern sensibilities. For example, there is a strong anti-body/anti-sexuality thread that runs through many of these texts. The struggles of the apostles and their eventual martyrdoms are in almost every case due to their preaching of the sinfulness of the conjugal life and their manifest success in persuading women of the rightness of their arguments. An extreme, to the point of ludicrous example of this is found in the *Acts of Thomas* 12–15,

Figure 16

where Thomas bursts into the bridal chamber of a newly married man and woman and warns them of the dangers, pitfalls and sorrows of having children! This recital of woe is so negative as regards parenthood that it is funny, provided one has a warped sense of humor.

On a more serious note, certain acts display doctrinal peculiarities. For example, the *Acts of John* displays tendencies toward docetic Christology, a heretical theology in which the earthly life of Jesus is regarded as merely an appearance, phantom-like and unreal—because, after all, how can a *god* be contained in flesh? As a case in point one can cite *Acts of John* 93 in which Jesus' body is ghost-like and he walks leaving no footprints or *Acts of John* 97 where Jesus' death on the cross seems to be in appearance only. Again, we do well to remember that the apocryphal acts represent antiquated theology best described as snapshots of theological "fads" that had their day. For all these blemishes, I am convinced that the joy of reading such literature greatly overwhelms any displeasure caused by issues of peculiar practice or poor doctrine. Simply put, the good far outweighs the bad. With this background in place, we can now focus our attention on one particular story known to us from the vast corpus of apocryphal literature.

In the years that I have spent studying the legends the early Church told about the apostles I have never encountered a story that has had a greater and more lasting impact on me that the "*Domine, quo vadis*" story. The story is found in the apocryphal *Acts of Peter* 35. The larger context for the tale is the city of Rome, during the reign of the Emperor Nero. According to the story, Peter had been preaching a "doctrine of purity," a doctrine whose tenants are never actually articulated for the reader. The text merely describes the reaction of Peter's hearers to his message. First, we are told that four concubines named Agrippina, Nicaria, Euphemia and Doris hear Peter and agree among themselves to "remain in purity," choosing not to have sexual relations with their master, Agrippa. According to the story, this Agrippa was a Roman prefect, an official of equestrian rank, the second tier of Roman society, just below the senatorial class. It was this office that was held by another famous "villain" in the Christian compendium of stories, Pontius Pilate.

To make matters worse, the *Acts of Peter* tell us that a woman named Xanthippe, the wife of an important man named Albinus, described by the author as a "friend of Caesar," responded to Peter's preaching in a way not unlike the four concubines of Agrippa. She also decided to forego conjugal relations with Albinus. Filled with indignation and no small amount of frustration, Albinus comes before Agrippa and explains his situation. Agrippa listens to Albinus' story and shares his own similar situation, along with the news that many other Roman men have also lost their wives. Hearing that his circumstance was more than common, Albinus explodes. He demands that Peter be executed as a trouble-maker. Albinus justifies his request by suggesting that he is making this proposal not only for redress of offenses endured but also as a way of defending the many other Roman men who have suffered similarly but lack the social position to defend themselves.

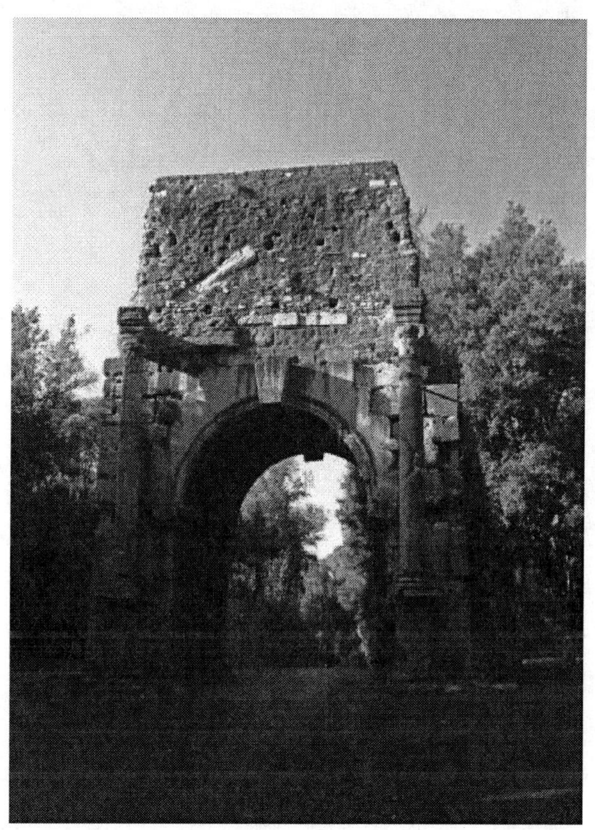

Figure 17

Somehow, we are not told exactly by what means, Xanthippe learns of her husband's plans and sends word to Peter so that he can flee Rome. When the rest of the Roman church learns of this danger, as one body they beg Peter to leave Rome. Resolute, Peter refuses to desert his charges. Undeterred, the community stresses to him that he is not deserting them but rather that he is "living to fight another day," i.e., so that he could go on preaching the Gospel elsewhere. Peter is persuaded by their arguments and consents to leave

Rome by himself. He dons a disguise and proceeds to leave Rome. A short time after he passes through the Gate of the City (**see Figure 17**), traditionally understood to be the gate located where the *Via Appia* runs through the city walls, he encounters the Lord passing by him, heading in the opposite direction, entering Rome.

Figure 18

Stunned, Peter stops and asks him, "*Domine, quo vadis*? (Lord, where are you going?)"

Jesus answers, "I am coming to Rome to be crucified."

Peter replies as if in a dream, "Lord, are you going to be crucified *again*?"

The Lord's response chills him to the bone, "Yes, Peter, I am being crucified again."

The mists part and the vision is gone, leaving Peter there alone, standing on the rough hewn cobblestones of the *Via Appia*. It takes a moment or two for the aftereffects of the mystical experience to wear off. When the fog lifts, Peter gathers himself and turns around, going back into Rome to meet his martyrdom. Today a small chapel stands on the section of the old Via Appia where this event is reputed to have occurred. Inside the chapel there is a section of the old road that has been incorporated into the floor. In the midst of the ancient stones is a small piece of marble with two footprints carved into it, marking the spot where legend says Peter turned around and reentered Rome (**see Figures 18–20**).

Figure 19

As I stated before, this story is particularly moving for me. To my way of thinking, it is a story about friendship, about broken promises and about second chances to make things right. In order to appreciate the power of this story, one must recall the image of Peter as it is presented to us in the canonical gospels. In our gospels, Peter comes across as a blue collar, working class man, fully aware of the harsh realities of scratching out a living under the thumb of the client king Herod Antipas, who in turn answered to his Roman overlords. The Gospel of Mark 1:16–18 presents Peter as a man who is quick to respond to Jesus' call to follow him and who is bold enough to express his opinion that Jesus is the expected messiah (8:29). Yet, this assertion is met with rebuke by Jesus as it more than likely reflects Peter's own militaristic views that Jesus has been designated by God as a new Joshua, who is destined to lead the Jewish people in a revolt against their political oppressors, both Jewish and Roman. The result of such a revolt would be to establish a truly Jewish kingdom in much the same way accomplished by Judas Maccabeus (see *1 Maccabees*) and his family. Some support is lent to this view by the Gospel of John 18:10 which relates a version of Jesus' arrest in the garden in which Peter is presented as drawing a sword and using it in defense of his Master. It should be noted that variants of this story appear in all four canonical gospels but only in John is the disciple identified; cf. Mark 14:47; Matt 26:51; Luke 22:50.

The portrait of Peter presented in the canonical gospels ranges from Matthew's strong support of Petrine authority (cf. the effusive praise of Peter in Matt 16:18–19) to John's innuendo that Peter's faith was wanting when compared to that of the disciple whom Jesus loved (cf. the foot race and subsequent response to the empty tomb in John 20:2–10; also see Peter's discussion with the Lord on the shore of the Sea of Tiberias in 21:15–23). The truth is surely somewhere in the middle. Peter's was hardly a perfect man. No such animal exists. If Paul is to be believed, Peter was inconsistent and weak in his actions regarding Gentile Christians and the use of Jewish kosher practices in Antioch (see Gal 2:11–12). Paul confronted Peter on the issue and never tells us that he convinced Peter of the error of his ways. Not long after this confrontation, Paul left Antioch for points west, never to return. Clearly, Peter was a formidable foe.

For our purposes, however, it is most profitable to consider the dialogue between Jesus and Peter as it appears in Mark 14:26–31. The scene is set in verse 26, which describes the following conversation as taking place as Jesus and the disciples walk out to the Mount of Olives outside Jerusalem:

> When they had sung the hymn, they went out to the Mount of Olives. And Jesus said to them, "You will all become deserters; for it is written, 'I will strike the shepherd, and the sheep will be scattered.' But after I am raised up, I will go before you to Galilee." Peter said to him, "Even though all become deserters, I will not." Jesus said to him, "Truly I tell you, this day, this very night, before the cock crows twice, you will deny me three times." But he said vehemently, "Even though I must die with you, I will not deny you." And all of them said the same. (NRSV)

We know how that all worked out. Mark 14:50 tells us that when push came to shove "the disciples all deserted him and ran away." Later, in 14:54, we find that Peter has recovered enough to follow Jesus "at a distance right into the high priest's courtyard." However, when questioned about his relationship with Jesus by those huddled around the fire, he cannot stand firm and denies Jesus just as his Master predicted. The cock crows and "Peter remembered." The last the reader sees of Peter, he is in tears (14:72; **see Figure 21**).

Figure 20

The Greek word ἀναμιμνῄσκω or *anamimnēskō* "to remember or recall to mind" is important to our story. It is my belief that this singular failure marked Peter in a profound way. He had made a promise to his friend and, at the very moment when his friend needed him the most, he failed him. There is a profound bitterness and regret that comes with that kind of collapse of trust between good friends. Clearly, Peter felt remorse but, as we all know, in life there are certain things that once done, cannot be undone.

It is claimed by some that the "feed my lambs, tend my sheep" exchange found in John 21:15–17 is an attempt at rehabilitating Peter, as if Jesus is somehow making Peter atone for his threefold denial. This may or may not be true but somehow I believe that any healing between Jesus and Peter is almost secondary to that needed within Peter himself. I suspect that the personal damage done to Peter's own trust in himself, as far as exactly who he conceived himself to be vis-á-vis Jesus, would be much more difficult to repair. We tend to carry the scars of our big failures longer and hold them more deeply and often only a profound act of atonement can give a sense of freedom.

Figure 21

I think of this word "remember" as it applies to Peter when I read the homily Peter addresses to the shaky young Roman church in the apocryphal *Acts of Peter* 7. As the story goes, Paul had been present with the Christians in Rome but had felt God's call to travel to Spain so as to spread the gospel. Shortly after his departure, the arch heretic, Simon Magus, who first appears in the canonical Acts of the Apostles, manages to lead astray the vast majority of the Roman congregation, causing them to look to him and not Jesus Christ as the one sent from God. As a response to the desperate prayers of the few Roman Christians who remained faithful, God sends a vision to Peter who, at the time, was staying in Jerusalem and instructs him to go to Rome. On his arrival in Rome, Peter speaks to the apostate Roman Christians who have gathered upon hearing that God had sent him to Rome to refute Simon Magus.

It is interesting to me that in this speech, Peter holds himself up as an example of an apostate follower of Jesus. He states clearly that he had been with Jesus during his earthly ministry and yet had fallen. He uses the reality of Jesus' forgiveness of his grievous error as a guarantee of his claim that Jesus would offer this same forgiveness to any who asked for it. He says,

> Dearest brethren, I denied our Lord Jesus Christ, and not once only, but three times. For there were wicked dogs who came about me, as said the prophet of the Lord. But the Lord did not lay it to my charge; he turned to me and had compassion on the weakness of my faith, because I was made senseless by the devil and did not keep my Lord's word in mind. And now I tell you, men and brethren, who have come together in the name of Jesus Christ: Satan the deceiver points his arrows at you too, that you may depart from the way. But do not be disloyal, brethren, nor let your spirit fall, but be strong and stand fast and do not doubt. For if Satan overthrew me, whom the Lord held in such great honor, so that I denied the light of my hope; if he subdued me and persuaded me to flee, as if I had put my trust in a man, what do you expect, you who are new to the faith? . . . Change your hearts, therefore, brethren beloved of the Lord, and be strong in the Lord Almighty, the Father of our Lord Jesus Christ, whom no man has ever seen, nor can see, save him who has believed on him. (Acts of Peter 7)

Certainly, we are dealing with early Christian legend. This is by no means a transcript of a Petrine homily. Yet, the ancient author clearly understands the human need to make sense of our failures, so that, in some way, our failures can be redeemed and have some value, even if that value is only in their ability to serve as an example of what not to do! It is this aspect of the picture of Peter, as it is presented in the apocryphal *Acts of Peter*, that appeals to me the most. This "Peter" has clearly spent time reflecting on his faults and failures and has thought both about what they mean to him as he moves forward and what they might be able to mean for others.

This brings us back to where we started, back to the "*Domine, quo vadis*?" story. In this story we meet an older, sadder-but-wiser Peter, who now understands how the world as a whole will receive his message. He now realizes that if he is to remain faithful to Jesus, there will be a price. He now knows that for a Christian the cross is not a possibility but a destiny. For a moment, he bows to the will of the Roman church, who merely seeks to save his life, perhaps in much the same way as he himself once did. However, after meeting his Lord on the *Via Appia*, the truth of what has taken years to learn comes back to him full circle. This time, he does not break and run as if he were a green recruit. This time, he stands his ground and faces down the enemy, knowing full well that this is his last battle. In doing so, years of nagging guilt, regret and shame melt away. Finally, he now can keep his promise: "Even if I have to die with you, I will never disown you."

Promise fulfilled.

That is what this learning module is really all about. It is intended to present its participants with the chance to consider the nature and depth of their own commitment to Jesus Christ and, perhaps, to choose a direction down the *Via Appia*. Will they continue south down the road or, like Peter, will they return to Rome? This is a question with which we as Christians must all grapple.

Rules for Playing Romans and Christians AD 64

Introduction

Romans and Christians AD 64 is an attempt to teach Church history through experiential learning. It is intended to teach the subject of martyrdom and persecution in early Christianity by immersing the participants in a situation that forces them to consider what their faith means to them and what price they are prepared to pay for this faith. Obviously, 'all analogies limp' and there is no way that we can really simulate (nor should we desire to) the brutality and horror of real persecution. However, within the context and safety of this game we can explore the subject of persecution and begin to address its relevance for our lives as Christians today.

Sadly, martyrdom and persecution are not subjects that are confined to the first several centuries of the Christian era, when faithful believers were faced with the terrors of the cross, the flames and the beasts. Modern martyrs abound. Among those who have bled for Christ in recent years are: Archbishop Oscar Romero (El Salvador, 1980); Archbishop Christophe Munzihirwa Mwene Ngabo (Democratic Republic of Congo, 1996); Bishop Juan Geradi (Guatamala, 1998); Bonnie Weatherall (Lebanon, 2002); Sr. Dorothy Stang (Brazil, 2005). The list could be multiplied greatly and grows almost daily. In light of this global reality, it seems irresponsible not to address this topic with American Christians.

Romans and Christians AD 64 is a "role-playing" game. By this we mean that it is a game that supplies its participants with "roles" or characters to play for the duration of the game. In short, all participants are asked to become actors and actresses in a grand drama. The game also involves the use of costumes and props and has "sets" where various "scenes" are enacted.

In general, the "drama" intends to recreate the events associated with the famous persecution of Nero in AD 64. With the city of Rome as a backdrop, the game is a struggle between the early Church (concretized at the beginning of the game in the persons of Peter and Paul and their immediate associates) and the Roman authorities (embodied in the persons of the Emperor Nero, the Senate and the Praetorian Guard). These opposing forces struggle for control over the hearts and minds of the inhabitants of the city of Rome. For their part, the Christians try to convert as many of the people of Rome as possible and form these converts into Petrine and Pauline churches. On the other hand, the Roman authorities act to crush the fledgling religious movement by capturing suspected Christians and putting them on trial for their faith. Those found guilty of being Christian are sentenced to death by crucifixion by Nero. More will be explained on the specifics of how this works later.

The game literally uses the metaphors of light and darkness (associated respectively with the Christians and Roman authorities) to symbolize the larger spiritual struggle that is implicated by this game. To accomplish this successfully, the game is intended to be played at night and requires a considerable amount of available space.

This game was created in 1993. Since that time it has been extensively play-tested with diverse social and ethnic groups and has held up very well. In addition, it has been used to teach participants from 6th grade to adulthood. While I originally developed this game with my 7th and 8th grade students in mind (typically 8th grade students study Church history), I have used it extensively with high school students, college students and adults. I have come to realize that it may best be suited as an intergenerational offering in which people of diverse ages play and experience it together. I have had many parents play the game with their junior high and high school children and they have reported back to me that as long as eight months later they find themselves discussing their experiences around the dinner table. As a Christian educator this is the optimum result: a faith experience that bonds families together and sparks familial faith-sharing and discussion.

Initial Questions to Help Set the Stage

What does role-playing mean in the context of Romans and Christians?

Role-playing means that participants are asked to "act." We ask that they do not play this game as themselves but that they literally *become someone else*, in this case a first-century inhabitant of Rome. To this end we supply each participant with a character card.

These cards are a basic outline of a person that either did or might have existed in Rome in the period of the mid-first century AD. Each card contains three points that help to explain the nature of the character and provide insight as to how the character might be played. The three character points are as follow: 1) *Character* (this provides the name and/or occupation of this person); 2) *Openness to Christianity* (this indicates the person's initial stance toward the Christian message); and 3) *Description* (this supplies the participant with a sense of their character's underlying motivation).

If you examine the various character cards that are included in this game, it will become apparent that there are a broad spectrum of characters and occupations. The characters themselves range from historical personages (e.g., Nero, Peter, and Paul) to those who are known to us only through apocryphal legends (e.g., Theon, Albinus, Quartus, Lithargoel, and Petronilla) to those who do not have names at all but merely represent people who actually made up the Roman populous (e.g., charioteers, slaves, the tavern keeper, and gladiators).

How are the character cards assigned?

Like any youth ministry event, *Romans and Christians AD 64* will require adult volunteers in order to make it successful. It should be noted at this juncture which specific characters should be assigned to adults *before* the night of the event.

It is my recommendation that any youth ministry program that wishes to offer *Romans and Christians AD 64* to its constituency should begin advertising it at least one month in advance. In addition, it is crucial that the overall event coordinator hold **a volunteer's meeting** at least two weeks prior to the event in order to 1) explain the game, and 2) assign the lead roles to adults who are able and willing to do them.

Based on long experience and much play-testing, I suggest that the following roles be filled by adults: Nero, the Praetorian Centurion, Peter, Paul, the three angels (Uriel, Lithargoel, and Thanatos), Simon Magus and Viterbius, the *lanista* (i.e., overall coordinator of the chariot races and gladiatorial games). These roles require some degree of preparation before the night of the event. *All other roles can be assigned randomly on the night of the event.*

What kind of volunteer should I recruit to play these lead roles?

The first step is to examine each of the character cards for the characters listed above. With even the most cursory perusal of these cards it is obvious that these volunteers should not be "shrinking violets." Certain characters such as the angels may be *non-speaking* roles, but they are important *action roles* in that the interventions of the angels are of utmost significance to the success of the game experience. You do, however, need loud, boisterous people that do not have a shy bone in their bodies to play characters, such as Nero, Peter and Paul! (I must state here that either a woman or a man can play *any* of these characters. In fact, in my extensive experience of playing this game, my most interesting "Peter" and "Paul" combination was the time I had two women play those apostles. Nero also has been played by a woman with good results.)

In the case of the key characters of Peter, Paul and Nero, I have created information packets to aide them in their preparation. This material is over and above the information provided to them by their respective character cards. With these three characters in particular you need to select volunteers who will do their homework and come prepared. Their actions are absolutely vital to the success of the event. If there is the slightest question as to the reliability of the volunteer I would urge you to choose someone who will take the time to prepare.

Peter

Peter must be played by a faith-filled individual who loves teens and is not afraid to embarrass him- or herself. This character must actually be prepared to preach the Gospel. If this game is to work, Peter must be a different character than Paul. I have always explained to those volunteers who choose to play Peter that the tone of Peter's preaching must reflect his personal experiences of Jesus.

Peter spent a significant amount of time with Jesus. In that time, he experienced a call on the shore of the Sea of Galilee (Mark 1:16–17), he witnessed the miracles, he heard the preaching and the parables, he was present at the Last Supper and experienced the shock of the arrest in the Garden. He denied Jesus and felt the twisting agony of the guilt that must have plagued his conscience. Finally, he experienced the amazement and awe of the Risen One. The content of Peter's preaching must reflect these *personal* experiences. This kind of personal tone can be achieved simply by reading the materials made available in the character packet included in this product and by retelling the stories in the first person (e.g., "I remember when Jesus had been preaching all day. We pointed out to him that the crowd hadn't had anything to eat and suggested that he send them away. He turned to us and told us to give them something to eat. Well, you can imagine how surprised I was! What could he possibly expect us to do? There were at least five thousand men there that day. . . .")

Paul

The same things that were just said about the kind of person you want to play Peter also apply for the character of Paul. The major difference between these two characters is that Paul is more "theological" in his preaching. Unlike Peter, Paul did not know the earthly Jesus. His experience is strictly related to the resurrected Lord. His writings in the New Testament include very little focus on events in the life of the historical Jesus. A key exception here is found in 1 Corinthians 11:23–26 where Paul relates the first available account of the Last Supper. This does not mean that Paul never told stories about the life of Jesus. This very passage indicates that Paul is merely repeating tradition that he has already related to the Corinthian church. His letters are occasional in nature and so do not accurately reflect the full sweep of his teaching.

Nevertheless, Paul's preaching should focus on the death and resurrection of the Lord Jesus Christ. Perhaps Paul thought: "Why focus on miracles when you can stress the Master's conquest of Death itself?" Therefore, Paul's preaching might sound something like this: "Jesus' death was for our sins so that we might be justified before God (Romans 5:6–11). We are saved through faith, not by any act of following legalistic rules and religious customs. The resurrection of Jesus can be viewed as a promise of more to come, a kind of 'first fruits' of eternal life" (1 Corinthians 15:20–28). Thus Paul's focus could be said to be on the significance of Jesus' death (1 Corinthians 2:2) and resurrection for believers in particular and for the cosmos in general (Romans 8:19–25).

Nero

The volunteer who plays Nero must be comfortable playing the "bad guy." This sounds like a given, but it's important to stress that the person who plays this part must have the stomach to do what is necessary for the sake of the game. Obviously, he or she will be a committed Christian who must, for the sake of the learning experience, stand for everything that is contrary to their faith. This is harder than one might first imagine, as the temptation for this person might be to be gentle, sympathetic or soft on the Christians. This is not helpful for the purposes of this game.

This said, the ways that volunteers have *interpreted* the character of Nero has had many variations over the years. Nero has been portrayed as "*Darth Vader*" (a dark, ominous character who uses brute force to crush the Christians), "*the Joker*" (a maniacal sociopath who actually enjoys killing Christians), and even a spoiled little rich kid or a confused buffoon of a leader who can't understand why the Christians won't "get with his program." Regardless of how this character is portrayed, the person playing Nero must be a strong personality who can easily steal the spotlight from the apostles if allowed to do so.

The Praetorian Centurion

The person that plays this character must be a strong leader, as this character serves as a catalyst for much of the game's action. The Praetorian commander organizes the Roman troops by grouping them into units and strategizes about how to attack and destroy the Church. This is not as much of a speaking role as the roles of Peter, Paul, or Nero. It is an action role that must be filled by a person who, upon understanding his orders, acts definitively to fulfill them. More will be said about this character's role in the description that follows.

The Three Angels

Like the Praetorian commander, these characters are more about action than speaking. They provide needed balance to a game that, without them, would be slanted in favor of the Roman authorities. They serve to hinder, delay, irritate and frustrate the Roman leadership and military. Only those who are not afraid to act quickly and decisively can play these characters.

Simon Magus

Simon Magus is a difficult role. He represents the primary "religious opposition" to the Christians. He claims that he is God incarnate, come down to earth. It is his job to win converts to his point of view. He has general immunity from Roman persecution, unlike the Church, so many more possibilities are open to him. The person who takes on this role must be strong enough to stand virtually alone in Roman society. They must be a bit of a "ham" and charismatic enough to use personality and humor to advocate strongly and doggedly an apparently outrageous claim. This character is best portrayed by people who are very quick-witted and able to think fast on their feet. I tend to ask for the "class clown" type to play this character.

Viterbius, the lanista

This character is essentially a ringmaster in a circus. The person playing this role must have a commanding presence and a loud voice. In the midst of the "confusion" of the city of Rome, he or she must be able to organize entertaining displays for the Imperial authorities.

In general, it should be stressed that these characters fall into two categories: those who speak and those who act. Those who speak: Peter, Paul, Nero, Simon Magus, and Viterbius. Those who act are the Praetorian Centurion and the three angels. More will be said about all of these characters in the course of this description of *Romans and Christians AD 64.*

How many people are needed to play Romans and Christians?

Over the years I have played this game with a range of group sizes. I have played with as few as 25 people and as many as 220. The game itself is equipped with 110 total characters, although nine of these are designated as "adult" roles (e.g., Peter, Paul, Nero, Simon Magus, etc.). The disbursement of the rest of the characters (101) is as follows:

- 8 associates of the apostles
- 7 Roman Imperial authorities
- 17 Praetorian soldiers (including informants, jailor and executioners)
- 60 Roman people
- 9 arena characters (charioteers, gladiators, boxers)

In my experience the game is best suited for a group of 80 participants, although larger games do work. If the game is larger than 100, I recommend adding additional soldiers and Roman people. If the game is below 50, eliminate characters from the Roman people as well as one informant and several soldiers. *However, make sure to include all the associates of the apostles, all the Roman Imperial authorities and all the arena characters.* In regard to calculating the number of soldiers, I suggest having a number of soldiers equal to 10–15 percent of the total number of participants.

How Does the Basic Flow of the Game Unfold?

Time Frames

As with any youth ministry event, *Romans and Christians AD 64* should begin by gathering the participants and calling them to prayer. After that, it is time for a basic lecture on Martyrdom and Persecution in the Early Church. This presentation is intended to lay out the historical and cultural circumstances faced by the early Church and helps aide the participants in entering into their roles.

Sadly, lectures often get a bad name in youth ministry. However, in this case, it is essential to the participants' understanding of what is at stake in the game that they have a general awareness of this subject. Among other things, it is important that the group is taught about 1) the shadow cast across Christianity by the criminal execution of its founder; 2) the basics of the Neronian Persecution in particular (including the legends concerning the martyrdoms of Peter and

Paul that are associated with this persecution) and 3) the general crimes associated in the popular culture with this new religion. This information is provided as part of this game module in the form of a brief essay on martyrdom and persecution, which includes direct references to primary source material for further study to prepare a catechist, youth minister or event coordinator with the knowledge necessary to give this lecture. I have found that a lecture of 20 to 30 minutes is sufficient to lay out a decent foundation for game play. It is my hope that in the future, I will be able to raise the funds necessary to create a DVD lecture that can be used in lieu of a live presentation.

Following this presentation, the game must be explained. The rules are outlined in this packet. These rules are available in two formats: 1) this rulebook and 2) a DVD presentation that can be shown to the participants. It is important to stress here that if the event coordinator opts to use the DVD presentation to explain the rules of the game to the participants, he or she *still must know these rules in detail* so as to be able to answer the inevitable questions and requests for clarification that always follow such an explication of rules. The explanation of rules will typically require at least 35 minutes.

The final stage before the game itself is the ever-popular handing out of character cards and special costumes. Obviously, the character cards that are distributed at this time are the remaining roles (i.e., not Peter, Paul, Nero, etc. which would have been assigned in advance). These character cards can be distributed semi-randomly. (I say "semi-randomly" here as I have learned that most young teenage males do not wish to play female roles, e.g., the Empress.) For the success of the game, I have found that the event coordinator must supply certain costumes as well. Much more will be said specifically about costumes later.

The actual game is made up of three turns of thirty minutes each and one half turn of 20 minutes for a total playing time of one hour and 50 minutes. These turns are subdivided into two phases: *day phase* and *night phase*. In the course of a turn, the day phase lasts twenty minutes and the night phase lasts ten minutes. In all, the game progresses as follows: Turn 1: Day Phase (20 minutes)/ Night Phase (10 minutes); Turn Two: Day Phase (20 minutes)/ Night Phase (10 minutes); Turn Three: Day Phase (20 minutes)/ Night Phase (10 minutes); and Turn Four: Day Phase (20 minutes). Finally, the event coordinator should re-gather the participants for sharing and discussion of the evening's experiences.

In all, it is safe to assume that the game will require just over three and a half hours to play, including all the elements described above: prayer, historical lecture, explanation of rules, questions and answers, character card and costume distribution, the three and a half game turns and a follow-up discussion. I have found that it is best to plan for four full hours for this event so that there is no pressure to hurry and everyone enjoys the experience. I suggest a 7–11 p.m. timeframe. The 7 p.m. start allows for about and hour and a half setup and explanation time, placing the actual game start time at 8:30 p.m. or later. Be mindful of the time of sunset. It is imperative for optimal game play that the sun be fully set before the game begins. Obviously, during late fall, winter and early spring, this is less of an issue as opposed to offering this game during the summer months. Saturday evenings seem to work best in my experience.

Locales and "Sets" for the Game

Romans and Christians AD 64 requires a considerable amount of space to play. Typically, I have organized this game in Roman Catholic grade schools and high schools or in Protestant churches with large facilities. It is a game that is intended to be played indoors, although on a number of occasions I have coordinated this game using several church buildings and it has worked quite nicely. In general there are two main areas in which action takes place: 1) the City of Rome and 2) the hiding places.

The City of Rome

The City of Rome is where all the actions associated with the *Day Phase* of each turn are played out. It is the *only* room that is illuminated for game purposes. It must be a large room such as a cafeteria or church hall and must be cleared so that it is open and free of clutter. I have used a gymnasium before but the acoustics are notoriously bad and I would advise against it if a better locale is an option.

The hall or room that serves to house the City of Rome must be set up with several areas in which various aspects of the game will take place. These areas are: 1) the Imperial Court/Senate; 2) the jail; 3) the tavern; 4) the arena and 5) the place of execution. For now, I will merely describe the location and setup of these "sets." Later, I will explain their functions in the game.

THE IMPERIAL COURT/SENATE The Imperial Court should be situated at the head of the room. It should include eight chairs, arranged in a semi-circular formation. The two innermost chairs should be different as they serve as the thrones of Nero and the Empress Poppaea. I recommend that these special chairs be bigger and more formal in character and that they be draped with purple cloth (an imperial color).

THE JAIL Choose one corner of the hall and square it off with tables or some other barriers, thereby forming a box. The "walls" need not be higher that one's waist as there are absolutely no "jail breaks" in this game. Roman jails tended to be subterranean and once a person became a "tenant" they stayed until released. Release usually meant death as a result of starvation or because of the horrid conditions or death in the arena. (See the historical introduction for more on Roman prisons.) The jail need not be much larger than a 12 foot by 12 foot square. The Jail is equipped with the character of a Roman jailor, Quartus.

THE TAVERN The tavern supplies the "munchies" (after all this is youth ministry we are talking about!) There is a character in the game that is designated to run this area (as well as slaves to help in the work) so you need not assign an adult to this locale. Many times, the City of Rome is located in a cafeteria or church hall that has a kitchen associated with it. This is ideal. Supply plenty of café-style tables and chairs for characters to come and socialize while in Rome. Think "coffee shop" here and you are well on your way. As for what the tavern serves: soda, chips, pizza, etc. Restrict the tavern to all things "salty." Nothing sweet (beyond soda) is to be served at the tavern. The reasons for this will become abundantly clear later. The Tavern should remain open through all *Day* and *Night Phases* of the game.

THE ARENA This is the base of operations for Viterbius, the *lanista*. I like to situate the arena in the middle of the hall being used as the City of Rome. As far as appearances, it should be an oval (marked out with orange cones or lined on the floor with blue painter's tape). The gladiator fights and boxing matches will be held inside the oval and the chariot race will be run around the outside of the oval. Simply put, Viterbius will use the arena to exhibit one event per *Day Phase* (i.e., *Day Phases* 1, 2, and 3, but *not Day Phase* 4). These events will take place while the Christian missionaries are carrying out their mission and, later, when the Christians who were arrested are put on trial and executed. The order of events in the arena (i.e., boxing, gladiatorial fights, and chariot racing) is determined by Viterbius or by the Emperor's request. The character cards of Viterbius and his or her assistant, Marius, the racemaster, explain all the necessary details of how the arena should work. See equipment lists for needed materials.

THE PLACE OF EXECUTION This area should be located either in an otherwise unused corner or alongside one of the outer walls of the hall. This is the area where those who are executed for their profession of the Christian faith are taken. This area should be provided with the following items: five pine wood planks (1x6x6; 1 inch thick/ 6 inches wide/ 6 feet in length) that will serve as crossbeams, 20 3/16 inch white solid braid nylon ropes of approximately 15 inches in length that will be used to tie the victims to the crossbeams, five plastic cups of water, a generous amount of washable clown makeup and a bucket of soapy water and old towels in case of messes. There is much more that needs to be said about this aspect of the game but that will happen later when the Turn 2 *Day Phase* is discussed.

The Hiding Places

Just as the City of Rome (i.e., the hall, cafeteria or gathering space so designated) is the venue for the *Day Phase*, so the Hiding Places are the setting for the action related to the *Night Phase*. Simply put, the Hiding Places should encompass virtually all of the rest of the facility being used for this event. For example, if this event is held in a church with a parochial school, it is usual practice for the City of Rome to be located in the cafeteria and the rest of the school (minus rooms such as the computer lab or key administrative offices) to become the Hiding Places.

As stated before, the metaphors of light and darkness are essential to this game. The City of Rome should be the *only room that is illuminated during the game*. To this end, the game should be scheduled when it is certain that the rest of the facility (i.e., the school for purposes of our suggested model) will be dark. Every effort should be made to make the facility as dark as possible. This means that many simple little things should be done (e.g., drapes drawn or blinds closed). However, it may also involve considerably more! It is highly recommended that the core team of those putting on this game visit the facility in question on some night before the night of the event. They should walk through the building, taking note of any areas that are illuminated by outside lighting, etc.

Once these problem spots are identified, it is important to recruit a sizable number of volunteers to show up at the facility hours before the event and cover these areas. In my experience, black garbage bags, rolls of black poster paper or some such thing work just great for this purpose. Do not underestimate the time needed to cover windows, outside doors, etc. The best way to do this is to recruit more people to help than you think you will need. A team of 10 to 15 people is more than enough for the job and will prevent the burden of the work from falling too heavily on any one individual.

If your facility has stairs, I strongly recommend that you purchase some small, battery-powered dome lights (i.e., the kind that are turned on by pushing in on the dome). Simply placing one dome light per stairwell will provide adequate lighting. It should be stressed here that during the explanation of the game it is important to point out the presence of these lights on the stairs and to urge the participants not to move or tamper with these lights. State that anyone caught doing so will be immediately asked to leave the event.

The Progression of the Game

Turn 1: The Rubber Meets the Road (or in our case "the chariot wheel meets the Appian Way")

Turn 1 begins with the Day Phase (as do all turns). The main objective in this phase of the turn is for the Christian leaders (i.e., Peter, Paul and their associates) to preach the Gospel so as to win converts to Christianity. Before the very first turn begins all those characters who are designated as Christians on their character cards (i.e., Peter and Paul and their respective entourages) should leave the hall and wait outside the room until the game begins. Once the Apostles are informed by the official game timekeeper (one of the angels) that Turn 1 has begun, they should open the door and enter the City of Rome, preaching the Gospel to all who will hear them.

As stated before, the apostles and their associates should interact with the people of Rome as if they actually were their characters. Peter should speak about his experiences with Jesus in the first person. The other Christians should testify of their own "conversions" to Christianity in a first person voice as well. The effect of this "internalization" of the Gospel message is quite powerful to witness and encourages the other participants to enter into their own roles with similar abandon. In addition, the varying responses that those initial Christians receive to their evangelical messages serves to unify those who do accept the apostles' message.

For the Christians leaders, the primary goals in the game are in the *Day Phase* to form churches from their new converts and in the *Night Phase* to keep these churches safe from Roman persecution. We shall now examine these goals in detail.

The Day Phase: Forming Churches Using the Three Apostolic Symbols

The Apostles Peter and Paul and their respective supporters should work independently to form a series of Petrine and Pauline churches. For the purposes of this game, a "church" is a Christian cell group of *no more* than five people, *including* the designated leader of each "church" community.

Before the game begins, at the time when costumes and props are distributed, both Peter and Paul should be given three "props" each: 1) several bottles of Holy Water; 2) a shepherd's crook or "crosier"; and 3) three pieces of Scripture. Each of these objects are important in the formation of their respective churches.

Holy Water for Baptism

As Peter and Paul and their associates preach the Gospel, some members of the population of the City of Rome will wish to "convert" and become Christian. Peter and Paul and their associates should use the bottles of Holy Water to "baptize" their new converts. They are to sprinkle the "catechumen" three times and use the ancient formula: "I baptize you in the name of the Father and the Son and the Holy Spirit" (see Matt 28:19 and also *Catechism of the Catholic Church*, hereafter *CCC* 232–33; 1239–40). Baptism can be performed by Peter, Paul or any of their associates and, later in the game, by their appointed successors (see *CCC* 1256). In many cases, those people who play Peter and Paul hand over the baptismal duties to their associates and focus their energies on their preaching and winning of converts. This is a good strategy as the main apostles have many responsibilities and duties to perform.

Once the new converts are baptized, they are to be grouped into cells of *no more than five and no less than three people*. If an odd number of converts is generated, then the churches should split off respecting the three-person minimum rule. Keep in mind, any original leaders such as Peter, Paul and their original associates must be included in this count as well. For example, if Peter and his initial associates (i.e., John Mark, Sarah, Petronilla, and Theon) preach and win eight converts during this first Day Phase, there would be thirteen total "Petrine Christians." (It should be noted that Paul and his associates would be at work in Rome trying to do this very same thing.) These thirteen people could be grouped in three churches as follows:

- Church 1: Leader: Peter, Sarah (now designated a "deacon"), Petronilla and two new converts
- Church 2: Leader: John Mark and three new converts
- Church 3: Leader: Theon and three new converts

"Feed my Sheep": The Crosier

Since the issue of leadership of these "churches" has been broached, the subject of the crosier can be discussed. The crosier is a staff with a hooked end like a shepherd's crook, carried by Christian bishops, archbishops or abbots, symbolizing their roles of caring for their congregations as shepherds who tend flocks (see *CCC* 881). In addition to the crosier's symbolic value of its bearer's role as "bishop", it also reminds its bearer of their responsibility to provide leaders for their communities. To this end, *Romans and Christians AD 64* has Peter and Paul appoint a single Leader or presbyter/ priest for each new church community under their authority and one "deacon" who they keep with them in their own home community (see the example "Petrine churches" above). Thus there can be as many presbyters/priests as there are churches but only one deacon in the Petrine churches and one in the Pauline churches. Obviously, there were many deacons in the early churches but I have chosen to limit the number for simplicity in this game.

I am often asked: "Who can be presbyters/ priests or deacons?" In many Christian denominations such questions are not an issue (e.g., the Episcopal churches have women priests and bishops). For Roman Catholics, this can be a very political issue. I have chosen to have no restrictions regarding gender and ministerial leadership in *Romans and Christians AD 64*. Political questions aside, since one can never know the ratio of males to females that will show up for this game it is simply not advisable to complicate things by setting restrictions that may be impossible to implement in a game situation. For example, if 70 people play *Romans and Christians AD 64* and 50 of them are women, it makes no sense whatsoever to impose gender restrictions on leadership for churches that are 90% women. The bottom line here is "playability" and my experience is that this is one area that best left open.

As noted above, the other significance of the crosier is its role of representing in a concrete manner the ongoing provision for leadership of the churches. Peter and Paul must understand that, upon their reception of a death sentence from Nero, they must pass on their crosiers to their appointed successors (either a presbyter/priest or a deacon). This is accomplished by Peter or Paul simply handing over their staff to one of their associates and telling them to "care for the sheep." It must be distinctly and clearly understood that the Roman authorities can *under no circumstances* take away or take possession of the two crosiers at play in the game. These two staffs represent the role of church leadership and the idea of Apostolic Succession (*CCC* 861–62) and, as such, are ephemeral concepts not subject to seizure.

The Scrolls of the Sacra Pagina and the Courier

The third and final props that are given to Peter and Paul at the beginning of the game are three pieces of Holy Scripture. For practical purposes these are the first pages of three books from the New Testament, photocopied and pasted onto a colored piece of construction paper. These papers are then rolled up into a "scroll" and tied with a ribbon. I recommend that for Peter you use the first pages of the Gospel of Mark, 1 Peter and 2 Peter and for Paul the first pages of Romans, Galatians and 1 Corinthians. I suggest that each apostle's texts be glued to a specific color of construction paper (e.g., blue scrolls for Peter, red scrolls for Paul). This helps to avoid confusion in the game.

These scrolls symbolize the Church's creation and preservation of the Scriptures. One of the objectives that Peter and Paul (or their successors) must achieve is *the exchange of these texts*. This exchange happens once per turn (i.e., three scrolls, three turns) and can *only* take place during the Night Phase. Before each Day Phase ends Peter and Paul (or those presently carrying their crosiers) must consult with each other as to where each "bishop" will be hiding during the upcoming Night Phase. Once the two bishops know the location of their counterpart's hiding place they must select a *courier*. Often the courier will be a trusted deacon or reliable associate. It is probably unwise to choose a new covert (for reasons that will be made clear presently). Once the bishop's church is securely settled in its hiding place and the Night Phase has begun, it is the courier's job to receive a single scroll from the bishop's hand and sneak unseen through the darkness to the other bishop's hiding place and deliver his or her scroll.

Snakes in the Weeds: The Informants

In the midst of all the apostles' evangelizing and building of churches there is cause for concern. In *Romans and Christians AD 64*, there are three characters called *informants* that may spell doom for the churches. These informants are unknown to anyone but themselves. For all intents and purposes, the informants are 'plainclothes' Roman soldiers who attempt to join the churches, only to betray them at the earliest possible opportunity. All the participants of *Romans and Christians AD 64* should know about the *existence* of the informants but no one (except the leader who is running the game) should know who is playing these characters.

It is important that when these parts are given out at the beginning of the game, it is done with all care so as not to reveal their identity to anyone. In fact, it may not be a bad idea to approach three reliable participants individually before the game and give them the informant's character card. The character card is clear about the role that the informant must play. The "how" of how the informant is to betray their church is up to the person playing the character. Some people have chosen to attempt to contact the Centurion during the *Day Phase* as the crowd mills about the City of Rome, passing on intelligence as to hiding locales and whatnot. Others wait until the *Night Phase* and betray their church's location by calling out to the soldiers. Still others "accidentally" get separated from their church and then find the soldiers so as to lead them to their fellows. Some "volunteer" to be the courier for their apostle, a perfect excuse to leave their church. If the informant is really effective as a spy, he or she can remain undetected by the churches throughout the whole game.

The Role of the Angel in the Day Phase

The Church is made of people and is heavily impacted by those same people's strengths and weaknesses. However, as Christians we believe that the Holy Spirit helps the Church (often in spite of herself). The angels represent the supernatural element in the game, God's continued intervention on behalf of God's people.

Angels are *always* immune to arrest. In addition, they have powers that enable them to assist the churches in both the *Day* and the *Night Phases*. In the Day Phase they can infiltrate the Roman Army Headquarters and spy on the Praetorians or stand in the Senate itself and listen to Nero's orders to his Senators and Praetorian Centurion. The angels are invisible and therefore cannot be detected by the Roman authorities. Therefore the Roman authorities must go about their business as if they were unaware of the angels' presence. Any intelligence that the angels can gather from their spying can be told directly to Peter, Paul or one of their successors.

Another key role of the angels is to try to detect the presence of the informants. If they observe any suspicious behavior on the part of those who are supposed to be baptized Christians they should report it directly to the apostles Peter and Paul or their successors.

There are two other special powers associated with the *Day Phase* that are unique to the angels, Uriel and Thanatos but they will be discussed later as the Turn 2 *Day Phase* is explained.

The Transition from Day Phase to Night Phase

Up until this point only a few things have been said about the role of the angels in *Romans and Christians AD 64*. However, their importance to the game should not be underestimated. All three angels have certain powers that are common to angels in *Romans and Christians AD 64*. These powers will be explained later. However, beyond these each angel has a unique capability that allows them to directly impact the game. At this juncture, it is important for us to consider the particular role of the angel, Lithargoel.

In addition to Lithargoel's normal angelic powers and responsibilities, Lithargoel serves as the herald and timekeeper for the entire game. As such this angel should be equipped with an air horn and watch (preferably a stopwatch). As stated above, each turn (including both *Day* and *Night Phases*) lasts 30 minutes. It is the angel Lithargoel's job to signal the beginning of the first *Day Phase* (by making a verbal announcement: "Friends, the Day is upon you! Use it for the greater glory of God!"). Each *Day Phase* lasts 20 minutes. Lithargoel must keep track of the time. When there are only five minutes left in the Day Phase, Lithargoel must announce this to the City of Rome and declare loudly: "Five minutes left in the *Day Phase*, Christians depart!" This serves as a 'two minute warning,' alerting the Christian churches to the approach of the Night Phase. Upon hearing this warning, the Christians then leave the City of Rome and head out into the darkened building in search of good hiding places.

Once the Christians have departed the City of Rome, the Praetorian Centurion should gather his or her soldiers and prepare them to go out. The angel Lithargoel should stay close to the Centurion as *only at Lithargoel's command* can the soldiers leave the City of Rome in search of the Christians. Once the remaining five minutes of the *Day Phase* have expired, Lithargoel tells the Centurion that he or she is free to go forth and thus the *Night Phase* begins!

The Night Phase: Keeping the Churches Safe from Roman Persecution

By the time that Lithargoel releases the Praetorians the Christians have had a full five minutes to locate their hiding places. This should be enough time for the churches to settle into the darkness and become quiet.

It should be stressed here that *no Christian should hide alone*. All Christians should have been assigned to a particular church (either Petrine or Pauline) during the *Day Phase* and now must hide along with the other members of that church. These churches (i.e., cells of no more than five Christians) should hide together as a group, not scattered throughout a larger area or the entire building. The only Christians who should ever be separated from their church communities during the *Night Phase* are the two couriers (one serving Peter, one serving Paul). Further, it is advisable that no more than one church should hide in any one hiding place (e.g., a classroom or janitor's closet).

Within minutes after their release, the soldiers will be fully engaged in their search for the fledgling communities. This search is hindered by three major factors: 1) the time limits of the *Night Phase* (i.e., a mere ten minutes); 2) the darkness; and 3) the activities of the angels.

The Arrests

Because of the limits of time and darkness, the Roman Centurion will need to maximize the efficiency of his or her forces. This will usually necessitate splitting up his or her soldiers into smaller units. To this end, the game provides the Centurion with two junior officers, an *optio* and a *contubernium*. These two characters allow the Centurion the option of dividing his or her forces so that they can cover more ground. It is a good idea for the Centurion to be very familiar with the building that provides the *Hiding Places* beforehand so that he or she can direct his or her subordinates to search specific areas. If one unit manages to find a church in hiding, they can send a soldier back for reinforcements or (in the case of a smaller building) simply call out for help.

If a unit of Roman soldiers comes upon a church in hiding *and actually detects their presence*—because of the darkness it is possible to pass by Christians and not see them—they should arrest as many as they can. However, when arresting Christians the Roman soldiers are bound by two unbreakable rules. First, each individual soldier may only arrest one Christian per *Night Phase*. This means that a soldier can only make three arrests during the course of the entire game. Second, a soldier must arrest the very first Christian whom he or she touches. Obviously, these rules limit the number of arrests and protect the churches from being devastated. For example, if a group of three soldiers comes upon a church in hiding, they can only take three of its members, leaving two behind. Since the three that the soldiers take is dictated by whom they touch *first*, the members of the church that was discovered may act to protect a key member (perhaps Peter or Paul) by throwing themselves into the arms of the arresting soldiers so that the soldier cannot arrest the apostle. On the other hand, when the soldiers detect the Christians in a room they may bar the door and call for reinforcements so as to be able to capture the entire church. As the soldiers make their arrests, they should lead their prisoners back through the darkness, to the City of Rome and deposit them in the Jail.

As we are discussing arrests here, it should be stressed strongly here that this is not a 'run and chase' game, it is a 'hide and seek' game. If this game is to be safe (especially with the darkness), it is crucial that participants not run. This means that the event coordinator and the adult playing the Centurion must stress to the participants that they are not to run during this game. When faced with arrest, Christians cannot run. It must be stated that this is not allowed. As an added precaution, it is wise for the Centurion to *reemphasize* this with his or her soldiers. The Centurion should state, "If the Christians run, you soldiers are not, under *any* circumstances, to pursue." *I have played this game over 25 times in 12 years and I have never had a participant suffer more than a skinned knee because I stress this "no running" rule.*

The *Night Phase* ends when the timekeeper, Lithargoel, signals the end of the ten minute period with a long blast of his or her air horn. If a soldier has not made an arrest before this signal, their ability to make an arrest for this *Night Phase* is forfeited and they must return empty-handed. Of course, they may make an arrest on a subsequent Night Phase if the opportunity arises. At Lithargoel's signal, the Christians may come out of hiding and proceed to return to the City of Rome without fear of arrest. Remember, no Christian may be arrested during the *Day Phase* or during their return to the City of Rome after the *Night Phase* has officially ended. All Christians must return to the City of Rome each *Day Phase*. It is inappropriate for Christians to remain in hiding during a *Day Phase*.

The Angels in the Night Phase

As with the *Day Phase*, the angels have certain powers that enable them to be of service to the churches during the *Night Phase*. First, they can aide the couriers in getting to their destinations by acting as a scout who warns them of dangers. Second, all angels have the ability to use what is called the "cloaking device." This power enables the angel to hide one and only one Christian per *Night Phase* in the folds of their garment in order to provide temporary protection from the Romans. This ability causes the Christian being hidden to become invisible. Even though the soldier knows where the Christian is he or she cannot do anything about it. They must move on to other potential targets. Lastly, the angels can act as heralds, going before the Roman soldiers and warning the churches of their approach, thereby helping to mask any noises being made by the hiding Christians.

Turn 2: The Christians Face Trial and Execution

With the beginning of Turn 2 comes the second *Day Phase* of the game. Everything that was explained about the *Day Phase* in Turn 1 is still in effect. The Tavern is still in operation. The Arena should exhibit its *second* show. The Christians should continue their work of evangelizing the City of Rome. New churches should be formed as necessary. However, at this juncture, several new elements will be added to the *Day Phase*. Once the following new ideas are understood and put in play, the game merely repeats these processes until it reaches completion with the final martyrdoms during the *Day Phase* of Turn 4.

The Trials

Now that there are several Christians inhabiting the Jail, trials can begin. Upon his or her return from the first Night Phase, the Centurion should report to Nero the exact number and identities of the Christians who were captured. If any of the Scriptures (i.e., scrolls) were confiscated they should be delivered over to Nero at this time. The Centurion should ask Nero if he is ready to begin trying the prisoners. At Nero's order, the prisoners should be brought one by one before Nero and put on trial for their faith.

As each prisoner is brought before Nero, they should be made to kneel. (Assume that even if they want to resist this act of submission, they are beaten down and ultimately forced to do so.) By now, either the Centurion or one of the other Roman officers (i.e., the *optio* or the *contubernium*) should have asked them their name and be able report it to Nero.

Nero should appoint one of the Roman Senators to act as a prosecuting attorney on behalf of the Empire. If Nero is so pleased he may choose to appoint another Senator as a defense attorney, although this is not necessary. The prosecution then begins to accuse the prisoner of various crimes, particularly the crimes typically associated with Christianity: cannibalism, atheism, incest, and hatred of humanity. These crimes are outlined in the historical section at the end of this book, in Nero's character packet, and in the character card of certain Senators. In addition, a discussion of these "crimes" and their meaning should be part of the lecture outlining the historical context of early Christianity martyrdom and persecution.

After these accusations are leveled against the accused, Nero must call the court to order and directly ask the prisoner if he or she is, in fact, a Christian. Nero must ask the prisoner if Jesus is indeed their "Lord" and "God." If they confess that they are Christian, Nero may summarily condemn them to death or attempt to get them to recant their testimony.

If a Christian prisoner denies that Jesus is their Lord or recants their testimony of Jesus at the coaxing of Nero and the Senate, they are immediately released and cleared of all charges. From the point of view of the Roman authorities they are free. However, from the point of view of the Church, they have committed the sin of apostasy, abandoning one's beliefs under persecution. At the point that this individual denies their faith, they are officially no longer a member of the Church. This is not to say that they cannot regret their decision and seek reconciliation. However, only one who carries the crosier (i.e., Peter, Paul, or one of their successors) can reinstate this person to full standing in the Church.

As for those who confess Jesus, they should be led off by the soldiers to the place designated for execution.

Execution

In *Romans and Christians AD 64* "execution" means crucifixion. This "crucifixion" involves tying a participant with nylon ropes to one of the five wooden planks mentioned above. At this time, any exposed skin (i.e., neck, ears, face, hands, legs, arms) should be painted with washable clown makeup. The game is equipped with executioner characters but *anyone who is not a Christian* should be invited by both Nero and the Centurion to help paint the Christians.

At this point it seems appropriate to note that even though it is advised that washable clown makeup is used for this part of the game there remains a risk that the makeup may stain the participants' clothes. For this reason, I suggest that when the game is advertised it should be specified that those who wish to participate should wear old clothes. I always repeat this warning at the beginning of the game as the rules are being explained and recommend that if any participant is wearing a new sweatshirt or article of clothing that they take it off and leave it in the Youth Room or some other secure place. It is good to go out and purchase several packages of simple white tee shirts before the event so that you have extra clothes on hand for those who did not see the warning on the advertisement posters or hear the announcements.

The Special Roles of the Angels Uriel and Thanatos in Day Phases 2, 3, and 4

As stated above, each angel has a power or ability that is unique to them. For example, Lithargoel is the herald who warns the Christians of the approach of the *Night Phase*. In addition, Lithargoel is the timekeeper and only Lithargoel can allow the soldiers to begin their search each *Night Phase*. The special powers of the other two angels will now be delineated.

Uriel

Uriel's power relates to his or her ability to aide the Church when in prison or on trial. Uriel is equipped with a "get out of jail free" card and a "reduce sentence" card. The "get out of jail free" card enables Uriel to free one person of his or her choice from prison and reflects the stories that are told in the New Testament book of the Acts of the Apostles concerning the dramatic rescue of Peter from prison by the angel (12:1–19) and the violent earthquake that freed Paul and Silas from their fetters in Philippi (16:11–40). It must be stressed here that Uriel can only free *one person during the entire game, not one person per turn.*

In addition, Uriel has a "reduce sentence" card. This ability enables Uriel to reduce one sentence of Nero. For example, if both Peter and Paul are arrested on the first turn. Uriel may choose to use the 'get out of jail free' card on Peter and then, after Nero has sentenced Paul to death, announce to Nero that he must reduce his sentence. The reduction of sentence has the effect that Paul would be sent back to jail for one turn and then executed on the following *Day Phase*. Thus, if Peter and Paul were arrested on Turn 1 (*Night Phase*) and brought before Nero for trial on Turn 2 (*Day Phase*), Paul's sentence would be reduced to give him until Turn 3 (*Day Phase*) at which time he would be executed. The purpose here is to simulate Paul's time in prison when he was known to have continued to build up the Church by his preaching and writing. Experience in playing this game has shown that an imprisoned apostle can do much to encourage and build up the churches as he or she preaches from prison. Of course, the Christians are allowed to visit their leaders and friends while they are in prison (i.e., stand outside and talk with them). Obviously, if Quartus the jailer is converted, these visits are facilitated even more.

Another way these two cards can be used is in tandem. For example, if Peter is arrested and brought to trial before Uriel can get to the jail. Uriel can use the "reduce sentence" card to put Peter back in jail after his death sentence and *then* use the "get out of jail free" card to free Peter. In deciding how to use these cards it should be remembered that both Peter and Paul were indeed martyred for their faith. I have seen time and time again how the death of an apostle can result in a strengthening of the resolve of the churches. Sometimes it is best to allow Peter and Paul to be martyred and protect the second generation of leaders that will take their place.

In this I am reminded of an incident that occurred once while playing *Romans and Christians AD 64* at St. Thomas the Apostle Parish in Grand Rapids, Michigan. The game began normally enough with the apostles and their associates preaching vigorously and winning many converts. Churches were formed and the new communities went off to hide. As expected, a decent number of suspected Christians were arrested, jailed and brought to trial. However, when these Christians were examined, a surprisingly large percentage of their number (perhaps 80%) committed apostasy. To the horror of the apostles (not to mention the local youth minister), the same thing happened at the second round of trials on Turn 3. At this, Peter (played by a friend, Christopher D. Alfaro, who actually helped me develop this game at its most seminal stage), full of zeal and righteous anger, strode forward and voluntarily gave himself up to the authorities. Everyone, including Nero, was stunned. When put on trial, Peter bravely and repeatedly confessed Christ and began to preach to everyone in the Senate. He continued to preach and sing songs as they led him away. Even when the soldiers and executioners were painting his face, he continued to preach to the assembled crowd, sing songs and, eventually, pray for the churches. His sacrifice electrified the weakened and demoralized churches. During the *Night Phase* of Turn 3, Paul gathered all the churches and as a body they decided that they would not hide. When the soldiers came upon them, they found them all kneeling right out the open, praying the Our Father in a loud, steady voice. As the soldiers took what they could of their number, the praying continued even more loudly. Not one of those arrested that Night Phase denied their faith. It was perhaps the most incredible thing I have ever seen in the course of playing this game.

Thanatos

The special role of Thanatos is hinted at by his or her name—the New Testament Greek word for "death." In addition to aiding the churches with the powers and abilities that are common to angels, Thanatos' main responsibilities are connected with the crucifixions that begin on the *Day Phase* of Turn 2 and occur on every subsequent *Day Phase* (i.e., Day Phase of Turns 2, 3, and 4). These responsibilities are twofold.

First, Thanatos must announce the "deaths" of the martyred Christians, ending their experience of persecution. In order to do this, Thanatos simply places his or her hand on the forehead of the martyr and announces that they are now dead and that no one may touch them any more. (This power of Thanatos must be explained at the beginning of the game when the concept of crucifixions is introduced. Thanatos' statement of death is absolute and must be respected by *all* participants *without exception.*) After making this announcement, Thanatos should proceed by taking the martyr or martyrs in question down from their crosses. The ropes that once bound the martyrs should be dropped on the floor and the martyrs led away to the holding room which should be designated as "Heaven." We shall explain this concept in detail shortly.

Second, while it should be recognized that in *Roman and Christians AD 64* the experience of "crucifixion" is pretty tame, it remains possible that certain players may struggle with the process of having their faces painted. There is obviously an element of ridicule and humiliation that comes with this experience, although this is by no means intended to be excessive or negative. I have found that the vast majority of game participants will laugh off any sense of embarrassment, especially since they are told what to expect in regard to "crucifixion" before the game begins. However, there may be a participant who, in the process of experiencing the game, takes this experience to heart in a way that is not good. (To put this in perspective, out of the hundreds of participants who have played this game I have only had two react in a negative way. I was told later that these students were known to have emotional difficulties. While their reactions were hardly traumatic, I did learn a valuable lesson. Now I make a point of bringing up this issue with the core team. If they have concerns about any specific students, we make a point to assign these students to roles that are less stressful and more "fun," e.g., gladiator, charioteer.) This is where Thanatos comes into play. Once the crucifixions begin, the adult playing Thanatos needs to make sure that the martyrs are his or her main priority. If any participant shows signs of undue stress, Thanatos should intervene immediately. This does not mean that Thanatos needs to have a "quick hook." As I stated before, the vast majority of the game participants have absolutely no problems with the face and body painting. Thanatos merely needs to be attentive and sensitive to the *possibility* that a participant may not be able to cope well with this aspect of the game.

Heaven

Until now I have not explained the concept of Heaven as it is conceptualized in *Romans and Christians AD 64*. Essentially, Heaven is a holding room where those who are martyred go to wait until the game ends. For the purposes of this game it should be expressly understood that *only martyrs* can go to Heaven. Furthermore, only Thanatos or—in the case of a turn in which there are many martyrs—another angel can take a participant there. Finally, it should be clearly understood that the existence and rewards connected with Heaven must be *a closely guarded secret*. Only the core team should know about its existence. As far as all the regular participants are concerned, when a participant "dies" in the game, they are merely taken to a holding room. In fact, whenever I explain the game, I state that the dead martyrs are taken to a holding room and are therefore permanently out of the game. These statements are *true*, just not *complete*.

How does this work? As stated before, when Thanatos or another angel takes a "dead" martyr down from his or her cross, Thanatos or that angel should immediately escort that person to the room designated as "Heaven." This room should be situated away from the majority of the action, preferably in an area of the building that has little or no traffic during the game. The windows of this room should be blocked out so that any participants who may pass by cannot see inside. Heaven should be staffed by at least two adult volunteers (preferably one of each sex) who are willing to supervise the festivities—as *hosts*, not military police! Remember, these martyrs are to be treated as heroes and heroines.

Simply put, Heaven is a full blown ice cream social. I recommend that a very good quality ice cream (e.g., Breyers) be purchased along with all the attendant toppings and things needed to serve this treat. (After all, what better way can there be to honor our new martyrs?) In addition, Heaven should boast a television and DVD/VCR with cartoons, standup comedy and/or music videos. I also like to provide cards and dice games such as Uno and Yhatzee.

On a practical note, it is wise to have buckets of clean water, sponges, soap, and plenty of paper towels so that the martyrs can clean up a little. Also, one should remember the old youth ministry proverb: "Where there is ice cream, there are many messes." Make sure that cleaning supplies are available and abundant.

Wrapping up the Evening: Gathering for Discussion and Sharing

As stated before, the Day Phase of Turn 4 is the final segment of *Romans and Christians AD 64*. Like the Day Phases on Turns 2 and 3, this Day Phase begins with the trials before Nero of the those Christians who were arrested during the previous Night Phase. Those found guilty are executed and then led to Heaven by Thanatos.

Allow time for this last group of martyrs to get their ice cream and clean up if they desire. Meanwhile, you can collect costumes and begin general cleanup. When the last group of martyrs has been served their ice cream, call everyone together and have them sit down on the floor of the room that served as the City of Rome. At this time have the martyrs rejoin the group. I usually like to have the remaining Christians and adult volunteers give the martyrs a standing ovation and cheer them as they enter the room.

Once everyone has been collected and the group has taken their places. I like to have a time for sharing. When I first started doing this game, I was a good little youth minister with a list of prepared questions that I would ask. I quickly learned that such things were largely unnecessary.

Now I just welcome everyone back together and then ask if anyone has any interesting story or experience from the game that they would like to share with the group. I find that I hardly need to ask. The participants are full of neat anecdotes, questions and feelings they experienced during the game that they are just itching to share. As might be expected, the trick is to remind everyone to really listen to what their peers are saying.

Over the years I have been amazed at the things the young people will say. I have found that there are several themes that seem to keep surfacing that are worth highlighting here. First, I regularly hear that those people who are playing Christians in the game experience actual feelings of fear and anxiety as they sit out in the darkness, hiding from the Roman soldiers. The people that have said this to me have included adults and teens, priests, brothers and sisters. They typically say something like, "I knew that this was only a game, but it began to feel real to me. Suddenly, I found myself praying for God to protect me . . . and I thought to myself, 'This is just crazy because its only a game, right?'" The second strand of experience is related to this aspect of a feeling of a compulsion to pray during this game. Again and again, I hear participants express that they found themselves praying, not just for themselves but for all the churches. Third, many of those who were Christians, especially those who faced trial and martyrdom, express a sense of strong emotion that came over them as they faced Nero. They repeatedly state how they realized that they had not been as serious about their faith as they should be. They express a realization that they had often taken their faith for granted. This sense of a "cost" for their beliefs is an area that is a rich source of ideas for discussion and sharing.

In addition to these serious statements, there will be plenty of "near miss" stories of how a church narrowly evaded capture. There will be humorous stories and many others that are worth hearing. I recommend that ample time be given for this sharing. Finally, the event coordinator should stand up and explain to the participants that martyrdom and persecution are not experiences that are unique to the ancient churches. As stated at the beginning of these instructions, there are many who have lost their lives for the sake of the Gospel in recent years. To this day, there are many places in the world where Christians face the very real threat of death for their beliefs.

I like to conclude the evening with a prayer for the Church worldwide, regardless of denominational differences, and especially for strength for those Christians who are suffering or in fear for their lives.

Equipment and Supply Checklists

The Game Locations

The Arena

- ❒ Styrofoam swimming pool "noodles" cut into 2 ½ foot length to use as gladiatorial "swords"
- ❒ Plastic shields (available at most costume stores) for gladiators (homemade wooden shields can be made with little difficulty)
- ❒ Cloth helmets for gladiators (costume store; be creative, have fun with these)
- ❒ *Optional:* If you want to be more creative (and historically accurate) with the gladiators, you can match a sword and shield fighter with a *retarius* (the gladiator armed with a trident and a fishnet). The trident (a devil's pitchfork) is easily found at any costume shop. Cut three 12 to 15 inch lengths of swimming pool 'noodle' and cover each of the three prongs for safety. A cargo net (for the top of a van or truck) should be available at any store that sells automobile supplies.

- ❐ Four plastic or wooden furniture dollies (available in either rectangle or circle); These sit about 6 inches off the floor and have plastic or rubber wheels. They serve as the "chariots." These are available at any home improvement store (e.g., Home Depot, Menard's, Lowe's).
- ❐ Four, fifteen-foot lengths of 1/2 inch or 7/16 inch twisted nylon rope. These ropes serve as the 'reins' that are held in the hands of the charioteer and loop around the waist of the slave who pulls each chariot as its "horse." These are also available at any home improvement store.
- ❐ The boxers should be equipped with "*Sock em Boppers*" (inflatable boxing gloves available at Toys "R" Us). Remember that these boxing gloves are not built for 300 lb defensive tackles. I strongly recommend for safety reasons that your "boxers" be the very smallest participants, preferably small girls. We never have had any injuries with this event. It is essentially a public pillow fight.

The Tavern

- ❐ Chips, pretzels, etc. (enough for estimated size of the group)
- ❐ Serving Bowls for munchies
- ❐ Paper plates and napkins
- ❐ Pizzas (frozen if facilities exist; delivered pizzas are also a good option)
- ❐ Drinks (2 liters of soda); ice and cups
- ❐ Paper towels and bucket of soapy water for cleaning up the inevitable spills
- ❐ Three long tables set up like a three-sided square to serve as the "tavern" proper

Imperial Court/ Senate

- ❐ Eight chairs for Nero, Poppaea and six Senators
- ❐ Two bolts of purple cloth (roughly the size of a single bed flat sheet) to drape over the two innermost chairs, designating them as "thrones"

Place of Execution

- ❐ Five pine wood planks (1x6x6; 1 inch thick/ 6 inches wide/ 6 feet in length) that will serve as crossbeams
- ❐ 20, 3/16 inch white solid braid nylon ropes of approximately 15 inches in length to use to tie the martyrs to the wooden planks (nylon is comfortable on skin and won't chaff)
- ❐ Five plastic cups of water (certain types of clown makeup need water to use them; e.g., the face paint that comes on a popsicle stick)

- ❒ A generous amount of washable clown makeup (various colors)
- ❒ A bucket of soapy water and old towels in case of messes

Jail

- ❒ Two long rectangular tables to be turned on their sides and used to square off the corner of the room used for the City of Rome
- ❒ A chair for Quartus, the jailor

Heaven

- ❒ High quality ice cream, toppings, cherries, whipped cream, etc.
- ❒ Plastic ice cream dishes and spoons
- ❒ TV with DVD/ VCR capabilities
- ❒ DVDs and/ or video tapes of popular cartoons, stand up comedy or music videos
- ❒ Dice and card games
- ❒ Clean up supplies for washing off makeup (e.g., cold cream; warm water; soap; paper towels)
- ❒ Supplies for cleaning up any ice cream related mishaps

Odd Supplies

- ❒ Several dome lights (battery powered) for placement on stairways (the number needed will vary with the site used but as a rule one per stairway will suffice)

The Costumes and Props Checklist

As part of your initial advertisement for the game you should ask that participants 1) wear old clothes so as to avoid the risk of stains from the makeup and 2) bring with them an old white sheet to wear as a Roman tunic. Other characters will need more specialized costumes and props. Most of these items can be found at a good costume store. A member of the church who has good sewing skills can easily make other things. Here are the lists for each character or group of characters:

Praetorian Centurion and the Roman Soldiers

- ❒ The Centurion should have a distinctive Roman soldier costume and helmet (costume store)
- ❒ Plastic Roman swords (eight to ten)
- ❒ Eight to ten cloth or heavy plastic Roman soldier helmets (Resist the temptation to go cheap here. If this game is to become part of your church's youth ministry or religious education program, you will need equipment that will last. The flimsy Roman helmets will be destroyed before the game is over and then, when you realize that you are going to play this game again, you will have to go out and buy the good helmets anyway.) The cloth helmet I use (approximately $30) is covered in a metallic gold fabric with a red plume made out of faux fur and is readily available at many costume stores, either on display or in their ordering catalogues.
- ❒ Eight to ten red capes (made of ordinary dark red fabric)
- ❒ Optional: I had a seamstress make about a dozen dark brown vinyl pullover-style Roman breastplates of various sizes. I found the costume pattern while visiting a local fabric store. Ask the clerk about "passion play" costumes. The internet may even be of help here.

Peter and Paul

- ❒ Two wooden crosiers (shepherd staffs); easily acquired at the local costume store
- ❒ Two robes (If you are Roman Catholic, merely hit up your priest for one of his old albs. Otherwise an old choir robe will suffice or something along those lines from a costume store.)
- ❒ Two pieces of colored fabric for accents on Peter and Paul's robes, one of one color, one of another
- ❒ At least four to six small bottles (for baptisms; two or three each for Peter and Paul when the game begins)
- ❒ Six pieces of 8.5 x 11 construction paper (three one color, three another) with the first page of the following New Testament books (for Peter: Gospel of Mark, 1 Peter and 2 Peter; for Paul: Romans, Galatians, and 1 Corinthians) pasted one on each of the six pieces (Peter's texts in one color; Paul's texts in another). These six papers should then be rolled up into "scrolls" and tied with ribbons.

Nero and Poppaea

- ❒ *For Nero*: Laurel leaf crown (costume store); white robe and dark purple piece of fabric to be thrown over shoulder for accent (only Nero, Poppaea and the Senators should wear purple as it is an imperial color)
- ❒ *For Poppaea*: Roman Empress' costume (costume store); beads

The Senators

- ❒ Each senator (six in all) should be given a ten foot long, six inch wide piece of purple fabric to wear over one shoulder (in addition to their toga) as a sign of their senatorial status. (A seamstress would be a great help here.)

Simon Magus

- ❒ A Black robe and a fancy jester's cap
- ❒ Magician's staff
- ❒ Magical items for "miracles" (costume store)

The Angels

- ❒ Three large white flat sheets (one for each angel). These sheets should be lifted over the person's head and pinned under the chin, creating a hood. In addition, the sheets should be pulled partially over each arm and then pinned at the wrist, creating "wings."

- ❐ A stopwatch or other timepiece plus air horn for Lithargoel
- ❐ Two cards (printed on colored construction paper) for Uriel: 1) "get out of jail free" and 2) "reduce sentence"

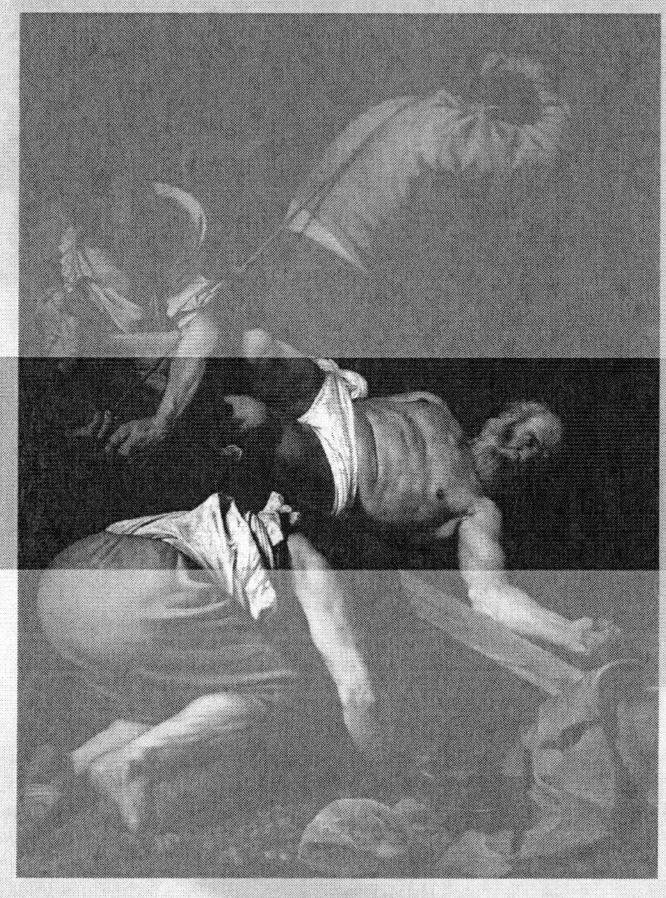

Preparation Packets for Peter, Paul, and Nero

THE FOLLOWING MATERIALS ARE collected as background materials for those volunteers who are chosen to play the roles of Peter, Paul, and Nero in *Romans and Christians AD 64*. These materials are intended to help the volunteer develop a "mindset" so that they can more fully play out their role.

All Biblical quotations are taken from the New Revised Standard Version of the Bible. It should be noted here that in the extended quotations from the apocryphal acts of the apostles I have used older translations that are readily available on the internet. By no means should these translations be regarded as the most authoritative available. Recent and reliable English translations of both the *Acts of Peter* and the *Acts of Paul* are accessible in Wilhelm Schneemelcher, ed., *New Testament Apocrypha, Volume 2: Writings Related to the Apostles; Apocalypses and Related Writings* (rev. ed.; Louisville: Westminster/ Knox, 1992). Further, a new series entitled, Early Christian Apocrypha, edited by North American scholars Julian V. Hills, Harold W. Attridge and Dennis R. MacDonald, is in the works through Polebridge Press. At the time of this writing the first volume in this series, *The Acts of Andrew* (2005), has been published. More volumes are on the way.

Character: Peter, disciple of Jesus

Openness to Christianity: Along with Paul one of the two major pillars of the Church

Description: After Jesus' death it is likely that none of the Twelve saw Jesus immediately (i.e., on Easter Sunday as most people assume). Various early Christian traditions state that the disciples left Jerusalem in a total state of disarray. Jesus' body was missing and rumors were circulating that some of the women had actually seen Jesus alive. But dead people don't just get up out of their tombs and, after all, these rumors were started by women—how reliable could they be? According to tradition, Peter went back home to Capernaum and basically tried to go back to what he did before he met Jesus—fishing. However, something strange and wonderful happened by the shore of the Sea of Galilee. Jesus appeared to Peter—alive. Despite Peter's denial (which was hardly much different than Judas' betrayal) Jesus offered Peter forgiveness. The world was changed that day. Peter's witness of the risen Lord was enough to pull the devastated disciples back together. The rest is history. Peter is sold on Jesus. He is beyond being worried about Nero and anything he could do to him. This character should be played with great passion and vigor.

A Character Sketch of Peter: Based on Selected Canonical and Noncanonical Texts

The Call of Peter

Matt 4:18–22 (NRSV)

As he walked by the Sea of Galilee, he saw two brothers, Simon, who is called Peter, and Andrew his brother, casting a net into the sea—for they were fishermen. And he said to them, "Follow me, and I will make you fish for people." Immediately they left their nets and followed him. As he went from there, he saw two other brothers, James son of Zebedee and his brother John, in the boat with their father Zebedee, mending their nets, and he called them. Immediately they left the boat and their father, and followed him.

The Transfiguration

Luke 9:28–36 (NRSV)

Now about eight days after these sayings Jesus took with him Peter and John and James, and went up on the mountain to pray. And while he was praying, the appearance of his face changed, and his clothes became dazzling white. Suddenly they saw two men, Moses and Elijah, talking to him. They appeared in glory and were speaking of his departure, which he was about to accomplish at Jerusalem. Now Peter and his companions were weighed down with sleep; but since they had stayed awake, they saw his glory and the two men who stood with him. Just as they were leaving him, Peter said to Jesus, "Master, it is good for us to be here; let us make three dwellings, one for you, one for Moses, and one for Elijah"—not knowing what he said. While he was saying this, a cloud came and overshadowed them; and they were terrified as they entered the cloud. Then from the cloud came a voice that said, "This is my Son, my Chosen; listen to him!" When the voice had spoken, Jesus was found alone. And they kept silent and in those days told no one any of the things they had seen.

The Denial

Luke 22:31–34, 54–62 (NRSV)

"Simon, Simon, listen! Satan has demanded to sift all of you like wheat, but I have prayed for you that your own faith may not fail; and you, when once you have turned back, strengthen your brothers." And he said to him, "Lord, I am ready to go with you to prison and to death!" Jesus said, "I tell you, Peter, the cock will not crow this day, until you have denied three times that you know me."

Then they seized him and led him away, bringing him into the high priest's house. But Peter was following at a distance. When they had kindled a fire in the middle of the courtyard and sat down together, Peter sat among them. Then a servant-girl, seeing him in the firelight, stared at him and said, "This man also was with him." But he denied it, saying, "Woman, I do not know him." A little later someone else, on seeing him, said, "You also are one of them." But Peter said, "Man, I am not!" Then about an hour later still another kept insisting, "Surely this man also was with him; for he is a Galilean." But Peter said, "Man, I do not know what you are talking about!" At that moment, while he was still speaking, the cock crowed. The Lord turned and looked at Peter. Then Peter remembered the word of the Lord, how he had said to him, "Before the cock crows today, you will deny me three times." And he went out and wept bitterly.

The Appearance of the Risen Lord
John 21:1–19 (NRSV)

After these things Jesus showed himself again to the disciples by the Sea of Tiberias; and he showed himself in this way. Gathered there together were Simon Peter, Thomas called the Twin, Nathanael of Cana in Galilee, the sons of Zebedee, and two others of his disciples. Simon Peter said to them, "I am going fishing." They said to him, "We will go with you." They went out and got into the boat, but that night they caught nothing. Just after daybreak, Jesus stood on the beach; but the disciples did not know that it was Jesus. Jesus said to them, "Children, you have no fish, have you?" They answered him, "No." He said to them, "Cast the net to the right side of the boat, and you will find some." So they cast it, and now they were not able to haul it in because there were so many fish. That disciple whom Jesus loved said to Peter, "It is the Lord!" When Simon Peter heard that it was the Lord, he put on some clothes, for he was naked, and jumped into the sea. But the other disciples came in the boat, dragging the net full of fish, for they were not far from the land, only about a hundred yards off. When they had gone ashore, they saw a charcoal fire there, with fish on it, and bread. Jesus said to them, "Bring some of the fish that you have just caught." So Simon Peter went aboard and hauled the net ashore, full of large fish, a hundred fifty-three of them; and though there were so many, the net was not torn. Jesus said to them, "Come and have breakfast." Now none of the disciples dared to ask him, "Who are you?" because they knew it was the Lord. Jesus came and took the bread and gave it to them, and did the same with the fish. This was now the third time that Jesus appeared to the disciples after he was raised from the dead.

When they had finished breakfast, Jesus said to Simon Peter, "Simon son of John, do you love me more than these?" He said to him, "Yes, Lord; you know that I love you." Jesus said to him, "Feed my lambs." A second time he said to him, "Simon son of John, do you love me?" He said to him, "Yes, Lord; you know that I love you." Jesus said to him, "Tend my sheep." He said to him the third time, "Simon son of John, do you love me?" Peter felt hurt because he said to him the third time, "Do you love me?" And he said to him, "Lord, you know everything; you know that I love you." Jesus said to him, "Feed my sheep. Very truly, I tell you, when you were younger, you used to fasten your own belt and to go wherever you wished. But when you grow old, you will stretch out your hands, and someone else will fasten a belt around you and take you where you do not wish to go." (He said this to indicate the kind of death by which he would glorify God.) After this he said to him, "Follow me."

An Example of Peter's Preaching
Acts of Peter 7

And on the first day of the week when the multitude was assembled to see Peter, Peter began to say with a loud voice: Ye men here present that trust in Christ, ye that for a little space have suffered temptation, learn for what cause God sent his Son into the world, and wherefore he made him to be born of the Virgin Mary; for would he so have done if not to procure us some grace or dispensation? even because he would take away all offence and all ignorance and all the contrivance of the devil, his attempts (beginnings) and his strength wherewith he prevailed aforetime, before our God shined forth in the world. And whereas men through ignorance fell into death by many and divers infirmities, Almighty God, moved with compassion, sent his Son into the world. With whom I was; and he (or I) walked upon the water, whereof I myself remain a witness, and do testify that he then worked in the world by signs and wonders, all of which he did.

I do confess, dearly-beloved brethren, that I was with him: yet I denied him, even our Lord Jesus Christ, and that not once only, but thrice—for there were evil dogs that were come about me as they did unto the Lord's prophets. And the Lord imputed it not unto me, but turned unto me and had compassion on the infirmity of my flesh when (or so that) afterward I bitterly bewailed myself, and lamented the weakness of my faith, because I was befooled by the devil and kept not in mind the word of my Lord. And now I say unto you, O men and brethren, which are gathered together in the name of Jesus Christ: against you also hath the deceiver Satan aimed his arrows, that ye might depart out of the way. But faint not, brethren, neither let your spirit fall, but be strong and persevere and doubt not: for if Satan caused me to stumble, whom the Lord had in great honor, so that I denied the light of mine hope, and if he overthrew me and persuaded me to flee as if I had put my trust in a man, what think ye will he do unto you which are but young in the faith? Did ye suppose that he would not turn you away to make you enemies of the kingdom of God and cast you down into perdition by a new (or the last) deceit? For whomsoever he casts out from the hope of our Lord Jesus Christ, he is a son of perdition forever. Turn yourselves, therefore, brethren, chosen of the Lord and be strong in God Almighty, the Father of our Lord Jesus Christ, whom no man hath seen at any time, neither can see, save he who hath believed in him. And be ye aware whence this temptation hath come upon you. For it is not only by words that I would convince you that this is Christ whom I preach, but also by deeds and exceeding great works of power do I exhort you by the faith that is in Christ Jesus, that none of you look for any other save him that was despised and mocked of the Jews, even this Nazarene which was crucified and died and the third day rose again.

The Death of Peter

Acts of Peter 35–37, 50

And as they considered these things, Xanthippe took knowledge of the counsel of her husband with Agrippa, and sent and showed Peter, that he might depart from Rome. And the rest of the brethren, together with Marcellus, besought him to depart. But Peter said unto them: Shall we be runaways, brethren? and they said to him: Nay, but that thou may yet be able to serve the Lord. And he obeyed the brethren's voice and went forth alone, saying: Let none of you come forth with me, but I will go forth alone, having changed the fashion of mine apparel. And as he went forth of the city, he saw the Lord entering into Rome. And when he saw him, he said: Lord, where are you going like this? And the Lord said unto him: I go into Rome to be crucified. And Peter said unto him: Lord, art thou (being) crucified again? He said unto him: Yea, Peter, I am (being) crucified again. And Peter came to himself: and having beheld the Lord ascending up into heaven, he returned to Rome, rejoicing, and glorifying the Lord, for that he said: I am being crucified: that which was about to befall Peter.

He went up therefore again unto the brethren and told them that which had been seen by him: and they lamented in soul weeping and saying: We beseech thee, Peter, take thought for us that are young. And Peter said unto them: If it be the Lord's will it cometh to pass even if we will it not; but for you the Lord is able to establish you in his faith and will found you therein and make you spread abroad, whom he himself hath planted, that ye also may plant others through him. But I, so long as the Lord will that I be in the flesh, resist not; and again if he take me to him I rejoice and am glad.

And while Peter thus spake, and all the brethren wept, behold four soldiers took him and led him unto Agrippa. And he in his madness (disease) commanded him to be crucified on an accusation of godlessness. The whole multitude of the brethren therefore ran together, both of rich and poor, orphans and widows, weak and strong, desiring to see and to rescue Peter, while the people shouted with one voice, and would not be silenced: What wrong hath Peter done, O Agrippa? Wherein hath he hurt thee? tell the Romans! And others said: We fear lest if this man die, his Lord destroy us all.

And Peter when he came unto the place stilled the people and said: Ye men that are soldiers of Christ! Ye men that hope in Christ! Remember the signs and wonders which ye have seen wrought through me, remember the compassion of God, how many cures he hath wrought for you. Wait for him that cometh and shall reward every man according to his doings. And now be ye not bitter against Agrippa; for he is the minister of his father's working. And this cometh to pass at all events, for the Lord hath manifested unto me that which befalls. But why delay I and draw not near unto the cross?

And having approached and standing by the cross he began to say: O name of the cross, thou hidden mystery! O grace ineffable that is pronounced in the name of the cross! O nature of man, that cannot be separated from God! O love (friendship) unspeakable and inseparable, that cannot be shown forth by unclean lips! I seize thee now, I that am at the end of my delivery hence (or, of my coming hither). I will declare thee, what thou art: I will not keep silence of the mystery of the cross which of old was shut and hidden from my soul. Let not the cross be unto you which hope in Christ, this which appears: for it is another thing, different from that which appears, even this passion which is according to that of Christ. And now above all, because ye that can hear are able to hear it of me, that am at the last and final hour of my life, hearken: Separate your souls from every thing that is of the senses, from every thing that appears, and does not exist in truth. Blind these eyes of yours, close these ears of yours, put away your doings that are seen; and ye shall perceive that which concerns Christ, and the whole mystery of your salvation: and let thus much be said unto you that hear, as if it had not been spoken. But now it is time for thee, Peter, to deliver up thy body unto them that take it. Receive it then, ye unto whom it belongs. I beseech you the executioners, crucify me thus, with the head downward and not otherwise . . .

(From chapter 50) Peter gave up his spirit unto the Lord. And Marcellus not asking leave of any, for it was not possible, when he saw that Peter had given up the ghost, took him down from the cross with his own hands and washed him in milk and wine: and cut fine seven minae of mastic, and of myrrh and aloes and Indian leaf other fifty, and perfumed (embalmed) his body and filled a coffin of marble of great price with Attic honey and laid it in his own tomb.

Character: Paul of Tarsus, Jewish rabbi and one-time persecutor of the Church

Openness to Christianity: Along with Peter one of the two major pillars of the Church

Description: Paul is an all or nothing kind of person. He is extremely committed to Christ. Probably his biggest motivation is the fact that he at one time persecuted the Church. Deep down there may well be guilt and remorse and a powerful need to atone for his sins by working and sacrificing himself for the Gospel. Paul has endured virtually every kind of corporal punishment for the sake of the Gospel and has not turned away from Christ. Nero has no chance to break his connection with Jesus. At this point in his career Paul has developed into a powerful theologian. He has many authoritative insights into the meaning of Christ's suffering, the nature of the

Church and the freedom that salvation can cause in the human heart. Paul is passionate, yet intelligent. He is deeply concerned with the welfare of the churches he establishes. He sees himself as a spiritual father to these churches.

A Character Sketch of Paul: Based on Selected Canonical and Noncanonical Texts

Paul's Conversion

Acts 9:1–19 (NRSV)

Meanwhile Saul, still breathing threats and murder against the disciples of the Lord, went to the high priest and asked him for letters to the synagogues at Damascus, so that if he found any who belonged to the Way, men or women, he might bring them bound to Jerusalem. Now as he was going along and approaching Damascus, suddenly a light from heaven flashed around him. He fell to the ground and heard a voice saying to him, "Saul, Saul, why do you persecute me?" He asked, "Who are you, Lord?" The reply came, "I am Jesus, whom you are persecuting. But get up and enter the city, and you will be told what you are to do." The men who were traveling with him stood speechless because they heard the voice but saw no one. Saul got up from the ground, and though his eyes were open, he could see nothing; so they led him by the hand and brought him into Damascus. For three days he was without sight, and neither ate nor drank.

Now there was a disciple in Damascus named Ananias. The Lord said to him in a vision, "Ananias." He answered, "Here I am, Lord." The Lord said to him, "Get up and go to the street called Straight, and at the house of Judas look for a man of Tarsus named Saul. At this moment he is praying, and he has seen in a vision a man named Ananias come in and lay his hands on him so that he might regain his sight." But Ananias answered, "Lord, I have heard from many about this man, how much evil he has done to your saints in Jerusalem; and here he has authority from the chief priests to bind all who invoke your name." But the Lord said to him, "Go, for he is an instrument whom I have chosen to bring my name before Gentiles and kings and before the people of Israel; I myself will show him how much he must suffer for the sake of my name." So Ananias went and entered the house. He laid his hands on Saul and said, "Brother Saul, the Lord Jesus, who appeared to you on your way here, has sent me so that you may regain your sight and be filled with the Holy Spirit." And immediately something like scales fell from his eyes, and his sight was restored. Then he got up and was baptized, and after taking some food, he regained his strength. For several days he was with the disciples in Damascus . . .

Paul's Description of his Own Life and Background

2 Corinthians 11:22–28 (NRSV)

Are they Hebrews? So am I. Are they Israelites? So am I. Are they descendants of Abraham? So am I. Are they ministers of Christ? I am talking like a madman —I am a better one: with far greater labors, far more imprisonments, with countless floggings, and often near death. Five times I have received from the Jews the forty lashes minus one. Three times I was beaten with rods. Once I received a stoning. Three times I was shipwrecked; for a night and a day I was adrift at sea; on frequent journeys, in danger from rivers, danger from bandits, danger from my own people, danger from Gentiles, danger in the city, danger in the wilderness, danger at sea, danger from false brothers and sisters; in toil and hardship, through many a sleepless night, hungry and thirsty, often without food, cold and naked. And, besides other things, I am under daily pressure because of my anxiety for all the churches.

Two Examples of Paul's Preaching

Paul's Own Words

Romans 6:3–11 (NRSV)

Do you not know that all of us who have been baptized into Christ Jesus were baptized into his death? Therefore we have been buried with him by baptism into death, so that, just as Christ was raised from the dead by the glory of the Father, so we too might walk in newness of life. For if we have been united with him in a death like his, we will certainly be united with him in a resurrection like his. We know that our old self was crucified with him so that the body of sin might be destroyed, and we might no longer be enslaved to sin. For whoever has died is freed from sin. But if we have died with Christ, we believe that we will also live with him. We know that Christ, being raised from the dead, will never die again; death no longer has dominion over him. The death he died, he died to sin, once for all; but the life he lives, he lives to God. So you also must consider yourselves dead to sin and alive to God in Christ Jesus.

Paul's Address to the Greeks at Athens

Acts 17:22–31 (NRSV)

Then Paul stood in front of the Areopagus and said, "Athenians, I see how extremely religious you are in every way. For as I went through the city and looked carefully at the objects of your worship, I found among them an altar with the inscription, 'To an unknown god.' What therefore you worship as unknown, this I proclaim to you. The God who made the world and everything in it, he who is Lord of heaven and earth, does not live in shrines made by human hands, nor is he served by human hands, as though he needed anything, since he himself gives to all mortals life and breath and all things. From one ancestor he made all nations to inhabit the whole earth, and he allotted the times of their existence and the boundaries of the places where they would live, so that they would search for God and perhaps grope for him and find him—though indeed he is not far from each one of us. For 'In him we live and move and have our being'; as even some of your own poets have said, 'For we too are his offspring.' Since we are God's offspring, we ought not to think that the deity is like gold, or silver, or stone, an image formed by the art and imagination of mortals. While God has overlooked the times of human ignorance, now he commands all people everywhere to repent, because he has fixed a day on which he will have the world judged in righteousness by a man whom he has appointed, and of this he has given assurance to all by raising him from the dead."

The Death of Paul

Acts of Paul (Martyrdom 3–5)

Nero therefore went on raging in Rome, slaying many Christians without a hearing, by the working of the evil one; so that the Romans stood before the palace and cried, It sufficeth, Caesar! for the men are our own! You destroy the strength of the Romans! Then at that he was persuaded and ceased, and commanded that no man should touch any Christian, until he should learn thoroughly concerning them.

Then was Paul brought unto him after the decree; and he abode by his word that he should be beheaded. And Paul said: Caesar, it is not for a little space that I live unto my king; and if thou behead me, this will I do: I will arise and show myself unto thee that I am not dead but live unto my Lord Jesus Christ, who cometh to judge the world.

But Longus and Cestus said unto Paul: Whence have ye this king, that ye believe in him and will not change your mind, even unto death? And Paul communicated unto them the word and said: Ye men that are in this ignorance and error, change your mind and be saved from the fire that cometh upon all the world: for we serve not, as ye suppose, a king that cometh from the earth, but from heaven, even the living God, who because of the iniquities that are done in this world, cometh as a judge; and blessed is that man who shall believe in him and shall live for ever when he cometh to burn the world and purge it thoroughly. Then they beseeching him said: We entreat thee, help us, and we will let thee go. But he answered and said: I am not a deserter of Christ, but a lawful soldier of the living God: if I had known that I should die, O Longus and Cestus, I would have done it, but seeing that I live unto God and love myself, I go unto the Lord, to come with him in the glory of his Father. They say unto him: How then shall we live when thou art beheaded?

And while they yet spake thus, Nero sent one Parthenius and Pheres to see if Paul were already beheaded; and they found him yet alive. And he called them to him and said: Believe on the living God, which raiseth me and all them that believe on him from the dead. And they said: We go now unto Nero; but when thou diest and risest again, then will we believe on thy God. And as Longus and Cestus entreated him yet more concerning salvation, he saith to them: Come quickly unto my grave in the morning and ye shall find two men praying, Titus and Luke. They shall give you the seal in the Lord.

Then Paul stood with his face to the east and lifted up his hands unto heaven and prayed a long time, and in his prayer he conversed in the Hebrew tongue with the fathers, and then stretched forth his neck without speaking. And when the executioner (speculator) struck off his head, milk spurted upon the cloak of the soldier. And the soldier and all that were there present when they saw it marveled and glorified God which had given such glory unto Paul: and they went and told Caesar what was done.

Character: Nero, Emperor of Rome

Openness to Christianity: None

Description: Nero was the son of the conniving Agrippina who married her uncle Claudius in her quest for power. To attain the throne, Nero poisoned his step-brother Britannicus and probably "helped" the aging Claudius to his death. Later, when he felt threatened by his mother's power, he simply ordered her assassination. All this was politics. At heart Nero was a playboy. He preferred to spend his time drinking, having sexual escapades and trying his hand at acting and music. If his power is threatened he will crush anything in his path. However, his down to earth "humanity" (as evidenced to the masses in his interests in music, acting and entertainment) made him popular with the people and much of his military. He is without conscience, capable of personally cutting a man's throat and turning around and going out to the theater.

A Character Sketch of a Roman Imperial Authority: Based on Selected Historical Texts and Martyrologies

Keep in mind that the major crimes that Christians were accused of by the Romans were:

1. **Cannibalism**—This is related to misunderstandings and rumors associated with the Christian practice of Eucharist—eating the body and blood of the Lord Jesus.
2. **Sexual Immorality**—This is related to rumors that circulated about sexual license and orgiastic practices associated with Christian worship. These rumors may have been related to the Christian practice of calling each other "brother" and "sister," holding religious gatherings which were attended by both sexes and the traditional Christian exchange of the kiss of peace.
3. **Atheism**—This refers to the Christian refusal to recognize the validity (or existence) of any God but theirs. It is also a challenge to Roman piety which traditionally relied on appeasement of the gods for continued military success. Lastly, it challenged the emperor's supreme authority by denying him divine status, an intolerable affront to Imperial dignity.

4. **Hatred of Humanity**—This was a charge leveled at Christians because of their unwillingness to participate in numerous societal events due to moral or religious sensibilities. For example, Christians rejected the theater because of its sexually offensive themes. In addition, because they refused to acknowledge non-Christian gods and goddesses, they refused to attend many public banquets (often held in temples), the athletic games (games such as the "Olympic" events were always dedicated to the gods) and the arena (due to the acts of murder that were committed there). This made the Christians appear "standoffish" and arrogant.

The Martyrdom of Polycarp 9–11

(Polycarp, a second century bishop from Smyma, Turkey is brought before a Roman governor and put on trial for his life.)

As he was brought before him, the governor asked him: "Are you Polycarp?" And when he admitted that he was, the governor tried to persuade him to recant, saying: "Have respect for your age" (and other similar things that they are accustomed to say); "swear by the Genius of the emperor. Recant. Say, 'Away with the atheists!'" (*Editor's note: In the Roman mind, the "genius" was a higher power that creates and maintains life. It tries to influence his destiny for good and accompanies a man throughout life serving as a tutelary spirit—not unlike a guardian angel in Christian thought.*)

Polycarp, with sober countenance, looked at all the mob of lawless pagans who were in the arena, and shaking his fist at them, groaned, looked up to heaven, and said: "Away with the atheists!"

The governor persisted and said: "Swear and I will let you go. Curse Christ!"

But Polycarp answered: "For eighty-six years I have been his servant and he has done me no wrong. How can I blaspheme against my king and savior?"

But the governor insisted once again, saying: "Swear by the emperor's Genius!"

He answered: "If you delude yourself into thinking that I will swear by the emperor's Genius, as you say, and if you pretend not to know who I am, listen and I will tell you plainly: I am a Christian. And if you would like to learn the doctrine of Christianity, set aside a day and listen."

The governor said: "Try to move the people."

And Polycarp said: "I should have thought you worthy of such a discussion. For we have been taught to pay respect to the authorities and powers that God has assigned us (for this does not harm our cause). But as for the mob, I do not think they deserve to listen to a speech of defense from me."

The governor said: "I have wild animals and I shall expose you to them if you do not change your mind."

And he answered: "Go and call them! Repentance from a better state to one that is worse is impossible for us. But it is good to change from what is wicked to righteousness."

And he said again to him: "Since you are not afraid of the animals, then I shall have you consumed by fire—unless you change your mind."

But Polycarp answered: "The fire you threaten me with burns merely for a time and is soon extinguished. It is clear you are ignorant of the fire of everlasting punishment and of the judgment that is to come, which awaits the impious. Why then do you hesitate? Come, do what you will."

The Martyrdom of the Holy Martyrs Justin, Chariton, Charito, Evelpistus, Hierax, Paeon, and Liberian

Recension B, 1–5 (*Justin was a philosopher/ theologian who taught in Rome and was martyred around AD 165.*)

In the days of the wicked defenders of idolatry, impious decrees were posted against the pious Christians in town and country alike. This was intended to force them to offer libations to empty images. And so the aforementioned saints were arraigned before the urban prefect at Rome, a man named Rusticus.

After they had been brought before his tribunal, the prefect Rusticus said to Justin: "First of all you must obey the gods and submit to the orders of the emperors."

Justin said: "There is no blame or condemnation in obeying the commands of our Savior Jesus Christ."

The prefect Rusticus said: "What are the doctrines that you practice?"

"I have tried to become acquainted," said Justin, "with all doctrines. But I have committed myself to the true doctrines of the Christians, even though they may not please those who hold false beliefs."

"You miserable fellow," said the prefect Rusticus, "are these then the doctrines that you prefer?"

"Yes," said Justin, "for I adhere to them on the basis of a correct belief."

The prefect Rusticus said: "What belief do you mean?"

Justin said: "The belief that we piously hold regarding the God of the Christians, whom alone we believe to have been the maker and creator of the entire world from the beginning, both visible and invisible; also regarding the Lord Jesus Christ, the child of God, who was also foretold by the prophets as one who was to come down to mankind as a herald of salvation and a teacher of good doctrines. Now I, being but a man, realize that what I say is insignificant when measured against his infinite godhead; but I acknowledge the power of prophecy, for proclamation has been made about him whom I have just now said to be the Son of God. For know you that in earlier times the prophets foretold his coming among men."

"Where do you meet?" said the prefect Rusticus.

"Wherever it is each one's preference or opportunity," said Justin. "In any case, do you suppose that we all meet at the same place? Not so; for the Christians' God is not circumscribed by place; invisible, he fills the heavens and the earth, and he is worshiped and glorified by believers everywhere."

Rusticus the prefect said: "Tell me, where do you meet? Where do you gather together your disciples?"

Justin said: "I have been living above the baths of a certain Martinus son of Timiotinus, and for the entire period of my sojourn in Rome (and this is my second) I have known no other meeting place but there. Anyone who wished could come to my abode and I would impart to him the words of truth."

The prefect Rusticus said: "You do admit, then, that you are a Christian?"

"Yes, I am," said Justin.

To Chariton the prefect Rusticus said: "Tell me further, Chariton: are you a Christian, too?"

"I am," said Chariton, "by God's command."

The prefect Rusticus turned to Charito and asked her: "What say you, Charito?"

"I am a Christian," said Charito, "by the gift of God."

The prefect Rusticus said to Evelpistus: "And what are you, Evelpistus?"

Evelpistus, one of the emperor's slaves, answered: "I too am a Christian. I have been freed by Christ and I share in the same hope by the favor of Christ."

The prefect Rusticus turned to Hierax: "Are you a Christian, too?"

"Yes, I am," said Hierax; "I adore and worship the same God."

"Did Justin convert you to Christianity?" asked the prefect Rusticus.

"I have long been a Christian," said Hierax, "and ever shall be."

Paeon arose and spoke: "I am a Christian also."

"Who instructed you?" asked the prefect Rusticus.

"I received this good faith from my parents," said Paeon.

"I listened gladly to the teaching of Justin," said Evelpistus, "but I also received my faith from my parents."

"Where are your parents?" asked the prefect Rusticus.

Evelpistus said, "In Cappadocia."

The prefect Rusticus turned to Hierax:

"Where are your parents?"

He answered: "Christ is our true father," he said, "and our faith in him is our mother. My earthly parents have passed away. I came to Rome because I was dragged off from Iconium in Phrygia."

The prefect Rusticus said to Liberian: "And what have you to say? Are you a Christian, and do you also refuse to be pious?"

Liberian said: "Yes, I too am a Christian. I believe in the one true God, and worship him."

The prefect turned to Justin: "You are said to be learned, and you think you know the true doctrine. Now listen: if you are scourged and beheaded, do you suppose that you will ascend to heaven?"

"I have confidence," said Justin, "that if I endure all this I shall possess his mansions. Indeed, I know that for all those who live a just life there awaits the divine gift even to the consummation of the whole world."

The prefect Rusticus said: "You think, then, that you will ascend to heaven to receive certain worthy rewards?"

"I do not think," said Justin, "but I have accurate knowledge and am fully assured of it."

"Well then," said the prefect Rusticus, "let us come to the point at issue, a necessary and pressing business. Agree together to offer sacrifice to the gods."

"No one of sound mind," said Justin, "turns from piety to impiety."

The prefect Rusticus said: "If you do not obey, you will be punished without mercy."

Justin said: "We are confident that if we suffer the penalty for the sake of our Lord Jesus Christ we shall be saved, for this is the confidence and salvation we shall have at the terrible tribunal of our Savior and Master sitting in judgment over the whole world."

The prefect Rusticus passed judgment, saying: "Those who have refused to sacrifice to the gods and to yield to the emperor's edict are to be led away to be scourged and beheaded in accordance with the laws."

Letter 97 of Pliny the Younger, governor of Bithynia and Pontus, to the Emperor Trajan

It is my custom to refer all my difficulties to you, Sir, for no one is better able to resolve my doubts and inform my ignorance.

I have never been present at an examination of Christians. Consequently, I do not know the nature or the extent of the punishments usually meted out to them, nor the grounds for starting an investigation and how far it should be pressed. Nor am I at all sure whether any distinction should be made between them on grounds of age, or if young people and adults should be treated alike; whether a pardon ought to be granted to anyone retracting his beliefs, or if once he has professed Christianity, he shall gain nothing by renouncing it; and whether it is the mere name of Christian which is punishable, even if innocent of crime, or rather the crimes associated with the name.

For the moment this is the line I have taken with all persons brought before me on the charge of being Christians. I have asked them in person if they are Christians, and if they admit it, I repeat the question a second and a third time, with a warning of the punishment awaiting them. If they persist, I order them to be led away for execution; for, whatever the nature of their admission, I am convinced that their stubbornness and unshakeable obstinacy ought not to go unpunished. There have been others similarly fanatical who are Roman citizens. I have entered them on the list of persons to be sent to Rome for trial.

Now that I have begun to deal with this problem, as so often happens, the charges are becoming more widespread and increasing in variety. An anonymous pamphlet has been circulated which contains the names of a number of accused persons. Among these I considered that I should dismiss any who denied that they were or ever had been Christians when they repeated after me a formula of invocation to the gods and made offerings of wine and incense to your statue (which I had ordered to be brought into court for this purpose along with the images of the gods), and furthermore had reviled the name of Christ: none of which things, I understand, any genuine Christian can be induced to do. Others, whose names were given to me by an informer, first admitted the charge and then denied it; they said they had ceased to be Christians two or more years previously, and some of them even twenty years ago. They all did reverence to your statue and the images of the gods in the same way as the others, and reviled the name of Christ. They also declared that the sum total of their guilt or error amounted to no more than this: they had met regularly before dawn on a fixed day to chant verses alternately among themselves in honor of Christ as if to a god, and also to bind themselves by oath, not for any criminal purpose, but to abstain from theft, robbery and adultery, to commit no breach of trust and not to deny a deposit when called upon to restore it. After this ceremony it had been their custom to disperse and reassemble later to take food of an ordinary, harmless kind; but they had in fact given up this practice since my edict, issued on your instructions, which banned all political societies. This made me decide it was all the more necessary to extract the truth by torture from two slave-women, whom they call deaconesses. I found nothing but a degenerate sort of cult carried to extravagant lengths.

I have therefore postponed any further examination and hastened to consult you. The question seems to me to be worthy of your consideration, especially in view of the number of persons endangered; for a great many individuals of every age and class, both men and women, are being brought to trial, and this is likely to continue. It is not only in towns, but villages and rural districts too which are infected through contact with this wretched cult. I think though that it is still possible for it to be checked and directed to better ends, for there is no doubt that people have begun to throng the temples which had been almost entirely deserted for a long time; the sacred rites which had been allowed to lapse are being performed again, and flesh of sacrificial victims is on sale everywhere, though up till recently scarcely anyone could be found to buy it. It is easy to infer from this that a great many people could be reformed if they were given an opportunity to repent.

Letter 98; Trajan to Pliny

You have followed the right course of procedure, my dear Pliny, in your examination of the cases of persons charged with being Christians, for it is impossible to lay down a general rule to a fixed formula. These people must not be hunted out; if they are brought before you and the charge against them is proved, they must be punished, but in the case of anyone who denies that he is a Christian, and makes it clear that he is not by offering prayers to our gods, he is to be pardoned as a result of his repentance however suspect his past conduct may be. But pamphlets circulated anonymously must play no part in any accusation. They create the worst sort of precedent and are quite out of keeping with the spirit of our age.

Angelic Forces

Character: Uriel, Angel of God

Openness to Christianity: Servant of God

Description: You represent the supernatural element. The Church is made up of people and is heavily influenced by those same people's strengths and weaknesses. However, we believe that the Holy Spirit helps the Church (often in spite of herself). As an angel you are immune to arrest. You can aide the Church in a number of ways: 1) You can aide the couriers in getting to their destinations by acting as a scout who warns them of dangers; 2) You can infiltrate the Roman HQ and spy on their plans and warn the churches; 3) You can try to discover who the Roman informants are and warn the apostles; 4) You can follow the soldiers around and verbally warn the Christians of their approach; 5) The "cloaking device" enables you to hide one Christian per turn in the folds of your garment in order to provide temporary protection from the Romans; and 6) You are equipped with one get out of jail free card and one reduce sentence card. (See pages 14 and 15 of this manual for additional details.)

Character: Lithargoel, Angel of God

Openness to Christianity: Servant of God

Description: You represent the supernatural element. The Church is made up of people and is heavily influenced by those same people's strengths and weaknesses. However, we believe that the Holy Spirit helps the Church (often in spite of herself). As an angel you are immune to arrest. You can aide the Church in a number of ways: 1) You can aide the couriers in getting to their destinations by acting as a scout who warns them of dangers; 2) You can infiltrate the Roman HQ and spy on their plans and warn the churches; 3) You can try to discover who the Roman informants are and warn the apostles; 4) You can follow the soldiers around and verbally warn the Christians of their approach; and 5) The "cloaking device" enables you to hide one Christian per turn in the folds of your garment in order to provide temporary protection from the Romans. Besides these important powers and abilities, Lithargoel is also the "timekeeper" of the game. The actual game *Romans and Christians AD 64* itself is made up of three and a half turns of thirty minutes each for a total playing time of one hour and 50 minutes. These turns are subdivided into two phases: day phase and night phase. The day phase lasts twenty minutes and the night phase lasts ten minutes. In all the game progresses as follows: Turn 1: Day Phase (20 minutes)/ Night Phase (10 minutes); Turn Two: Day Phase (20 minutes)/ Night Phase (10 minutes); Turn Three: Day Phase (20 minutes)/ Night Phase (10 minutes); and Turn Four: Day Phase (20 minutes). Finally, the event coordinator must re-gather the participants for sharing and discussion of the evening's experiences. (See pages 11 and 12 of this manual for additional details.)

Character: Thanatos, Death Angel

Openness to Christianity: Servant of God

Description: You represent the supernatural element. The Church is made up of people and is heavily influenced by those same people's strengths and weaknesses. However, we believe that the Holy Spirit helps the Church (often in spite of herself). As an angel you are immune to arrest. You can aide the Church in a number of ways: 1) You can aide the couriers in getting to their destinations by acting as a scout who warns them of dangers; 2) You can infiltrate the Roman HQ and spy on their plans and warn the Churches; 3) You can try to discover who the Roman informants are and warn the apostles; 4) You can follow the soldiers around and verbally warn the Christians of their approach; and 5) The "cloaking device" enables you to hide one Christian per turn in the folds of your garment in order to provide temporary protection from the Romans. *In addition to the powers listed above, your primary responsibility will be to monitor the Christians being martyred for their faith. Crucifixion for the martyrs only means having one's face (sometimes also arms and/ or legs) painted but can still be rather intense. Stay near to the martyrs as they are being "killed," if they seem unduly upset simply touch them on the forehead and tell the Romans that they are now dead. Then take them down from their cross and lead them to the place designated as heaven.* (See pages 15 to 17 of this manual for additional details.)

Character Cards

The Christians: Associates of the Apostles

The Roman Imperial Authorities

The Roman Army: Praetorian Guard

The Roman People

The Arena

The Christians: Associates of the Apostles

John Mark

Openness to Christianity:
committed Christian

Description: You are the nephew of Barnabas, Paul's first missionary partner. However, differences of opinion caused both you and your uncle Barnabas to leave Paul and start off on your own. Later, you began working with the apostle, Peter. You are now his closest associate and refer to him as your "father," an indication of your love for him. Tradition says that you will eventually write the Gospel of Mark, a document, it is said, that reflects Peter's gospel preaching.

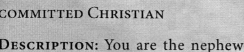

Timothy

Openness to Christianity:
committed Christian

Description: You are a companion and disciple of Paul. You are a native of Lystra, a town located in what is now south-central Turkey. Your father is Greek and your mother (Eunice) is a Jewish-Christian. You are very committed to Paul and have ministered at his side at Berea, Corinth, Philippi, Thessalonika, etc. Typically, you are Paul's messenger and representative. You have represented him to the churches at Philippi, Thessalonika and Corinth. At Paul's request, you have traveled alone into Macedonia, preaching the gospel.

Aquila

Openness to Christianity:committed Christian

Description: You are a dedicated companion of Paul. You and your wife, Prisca, are tent makers (like Paul) who originally lived in Rome but were forced to leave the city when all Jews were banned from Rome under Claudius. You traveled to Corinth where you first met Paul and helped him found a church there. Eventually, you traveled with Paul to Ephesus (in modern Turkey) where you continued to assist him in his missionary efforts.

Narcissus

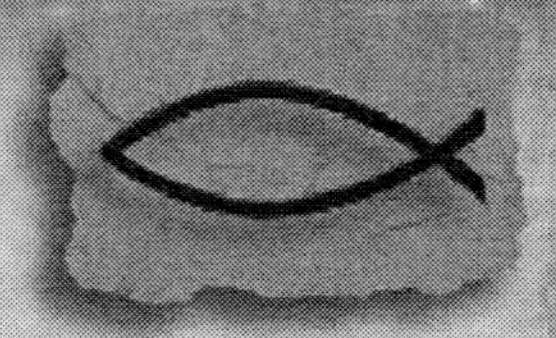

Openness to Christianity:
a priest of the Roman church, faithful to Paul

Description: You are a faithful leader in the Roman church. You support Paul's ministry and help further the work by heading up one of Paul's churches in Rome. One of your duties is to identify Simon Magus and make sure that Simon does not lead astray any of the new Christians converted by Paul. Be wary of Simon, he is not to be trusted. Be prepared to preach publicly against his lies and deceptions—the fate of the Church may be in your hands.

Prisca

Openness to Christianity: committed Christian

Description: You are a dedicated companion of Paul. You and your husband, Aqulia, are tent makers (like Paul) who originally lived in Rome but were forced to leave the city when all Jews were banned from Rome under Claudius. You traveled to Corinth where you first met Paul and helped him found a church there. Eventually, you traveled with Paul to Ephesus (in modern Turkey) where you continued to assist him in his missionary efforts.

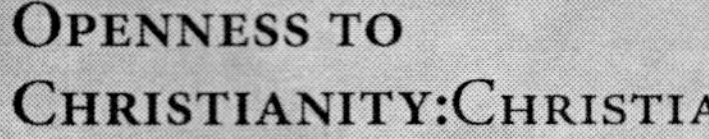

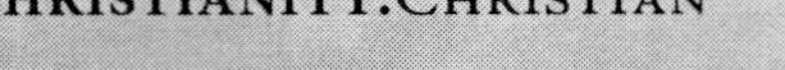

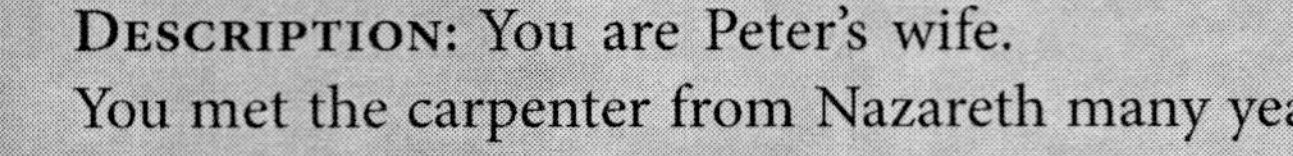

Sarah, Peter's wife

Openness to Christianity: Christian

Description: You are Peter's wife.
You met the carpenter from Nazareth many years ago when your husband fished the waters of the Sea of Galilee. Jesus came to your house and healed your mother, who was lying sick in her bed with an uncontrollable fever. You know that Jesus is the Messiah and support and aide your husband, helping him to preach Jesus' message of God's love for humanity. Now, along with your daughter, you travel from place to place with your husband, telling people about Jesus.

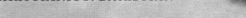

Theon

Openness to Christianity: Convert of Peter (already a Christian at the start of the game)

Description: You met Peter only a short time before the game begins. You were the captain of the ship that brought Peter to Rome. During that voyage you spent time talking with Peter and, eventually, converted. Peter actually baptized you while you were still at sea. You have left your ship and are now a companion of Peter.

Petronilla, Peter's daughter

Openness to Christianity: Christian

Description: You are Peter's teen-aged daughter. You were not even born yet when your father began his ministry. When you were only ten years old a rich man named Ptolemaeus wanted to marry you. You are your mother and father's youngest child and at the time she felt that it was just too soon for you to get married. She refused consent. The man kidnapped you and would have made you his wife by force if not for your father. Your father prayed to God to preserve your chastity. As a result of his prayers, you were paralyzed on one side of your body from your head to your toenails. You remain paralyzed to this day. You cannot walk. Only one leg and one arm are functional. You MUST have help to move.

The Roman Imperial Authorities

Poppaea, Empress of Rome

Openness to Christianity: Neutral

Description: You are the wife of Nero. Your life is a whirlwind of parties, drinking and sex. You have everything you could ever want. Sometimes, when you are all alone, you just want to scream. You have everything—so why do you feel so alone and empty.

(Information on Nero: To attain the throne, Nero poisoned his step-brother Britannicus and probably "helped" the aging Claudius to his death. Later, when he felt threatened by his mother's power, he simply ordered her assassination. All this was politics. At heart Nero was a playboy. He preferred to spend his time drinking, having sexual escapades and trying his hand at acting and music. If his power is threatened he will crush anything in his path. He is without conscience. Capable of personally cutting a man's throat and turning around and going out to the theater.)

You can listen to Peter and Paul. However, conversion to Christianity is incredibly risky. If Nero finds out, you are dead. If you do convert, you could be very helpful to the churches but the risk would be huge.

Gaius, Roman Senator

Openness to Christianity: Somewhat Open

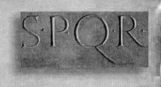

Description: You are a wealthy land owner. Since Nero's ascent to power you have seen a number of other senators killed because Nero perceived them as political threats. You fear Nero. At the same time you feel a gaping emptiness in your life. Your wealth is no protection against Nero's greed. However, you are not stupid. You will have to be convinced that Christianity is the right way to go. Therefore, you would be less open to the message of the illiterate Peter and more open to the educated Paul. The decision is yours. Feel free to ask questions of Paul. Make him convince you. If he doesn't, don't convert.

Vibius, Roman Senator

Openness to Christianity: Neutral

Description: You are a wealthy land owner. Since Nero's ascent to power you have seen a number of other senators killed because Nero perceived them as political threats. You fear Nero. Therefore, you are very cautious about doing anything that would put your life at risk. Publicly, you should denounce Christians as uneducated slaves and women. Make a point to show support for Nero's punishment of the Christians. (They deserve it as far as you are concerned. Anyone stupid enough to deliberately incur Nero's wrath deserves what they get.) Personally, you might be open to hear the Gospel. However, you would need Peter or Paul to personally speak with you and convince you. After all, you are an important person!

Marcellus, Roman Senator

Openness to Christianity: Neutral

Description: You are a Roman senator and wealthy land owner. You own a extravagant villa on the outskirts of the city (see the gamemaster for details). Since Nero's ascent to power you have seen a number of other senators killed because Nero perceived them as political threats. You fear Nero. Therefore, you are very cautious about doing anything that would put your life at risk. Personally, you are searching for spiritual truth. You are prepared to give a fair hearing to any philosopher or holy man. You are open to hear the Gospel. However, you must give equal hearing to Simon Magus, Peter and Paul. Then follow the one that most convinces you.

Agrippa,
Senator and Praetor (Judge)

Openness to Christianity: Hostile

Description: You are a Roman magistrate. You are a friend of Nero and can help in the trials of any Christians. Act as a prosecuting attorney. Here are some charges you can make against the Christians (the Christians were accused of four main crimes):

1) Cannibalism (they eat the 'body and blood' of a man Jesus; 2) Atheism (they believe in one God and ignore all the rest); 3) Sexual immorality (they greet each other as brother and sister with kisses); 4) Hatred of Humanity (they keep to themselves and don't participate in religious festivals and other civic events such as the gladiatorial games).

Albinus,
Roman Senator

Openness to Christianity: Hostile

Description: You are a Roman senator and close friend of Nero. You fear Nero. Therefore, you are very cautious about doing anything that would put your life at risk. Publicly, you should denounce Christians as uneducated slaves and women. Make a point to show support for Nero's punishment of the Christians. (They deserve it as far as you are concerned. Anyone stupid enough to deliberately incur Nero's wrath deserves what they get.)

Demetrius,
Roman Senator

Openness to Christianity: Positive-Neutral

Description: You are a Roman senator. You are wealthy, far beyond the wildest dreams of most of your fellow Romans but you are unhappy. There is something about Paul's message that strikes a chord in your heart. If you so choose, covert to Christianity and do everything in your power as a senator to help the Christian cause. However, beware of letting your sympathies become too obvious. If you are suspected of being a Christian, your fellow senators may well bring you up on charges. You have enemies in the Senate that would like nothing more than to see you banished from Rome... or worse.

Praetorian Centurion

Openness to Christianity:
None

Description: Career soldier. You are a simple man who, by hard work, long years as a combat soldier and luck, has risen higher in the ranks than anyone in his family. Your street smarts tell you to take orders and not to ask questions. As a soldier you show no mercy and expect none. As a person you are conservative and religious but your religion is old Roman.

Optio, (a Roman non-commissioned officer, second-in-command of a century [80 men])

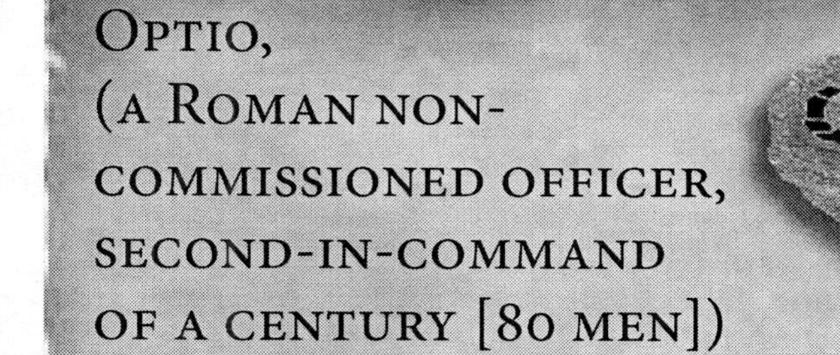

Openness to Christianity: None

Description: You are a battle-hardened veteran. You follow orders and don't question your superiors. You are directly under the command of the Praetorian centurion. If the Roman forces are ever divided, you will undoubtedly be given command of one of the detachments. Make yourself known to your superior immediately.

Contubernium (pronounced 'con 2 burn ee um'), Roman soldier

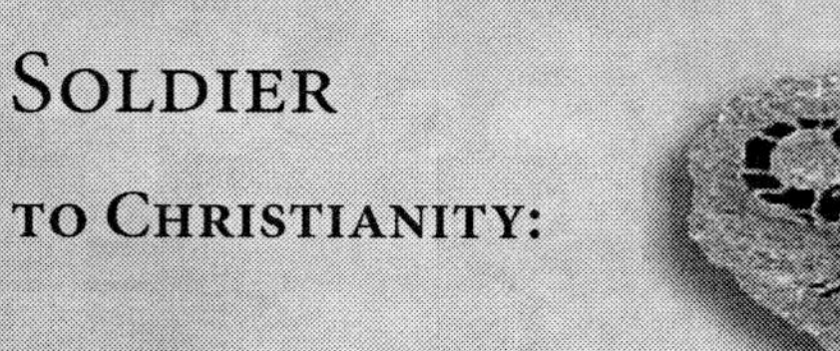

Openness to Christianity: neutral to negative

Description: You are a sergeant. You have been in the Praetorian guard for ten years now. You like the cushy life of a raetorian guardsman. You don't have to fight in combat, you get to live in Rome and the pay is better than any other unit in the Army. Make sure you make yourself known to the Roman centurion. He will most likely use you to head up a Roman Army detachment when you search for the Christians.

Roman Soldier

Openness to Christianity:
None

Description: You are a battle-hardened veteran. You follow orders and don't question your superiors.

Roman Soldier

Openness to Christianity:
None

Description: You are a battle-hardened veteran. You follow orders and don't question your superiors.

Roman Soldier

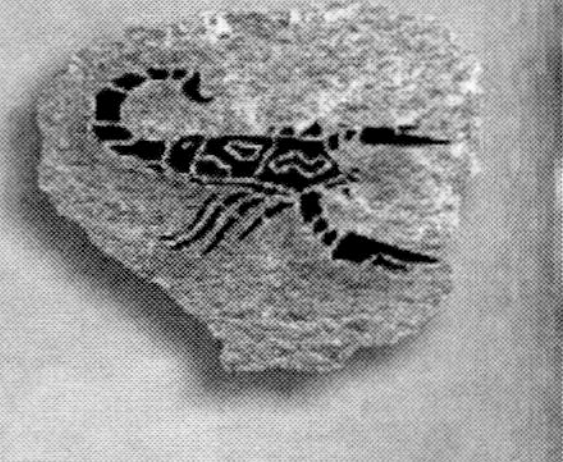

Openness to Christianity:
None

Description: You are a battle-hardened veteran. You follow orders and don't question your superiors.

Longus, Roman Soldier

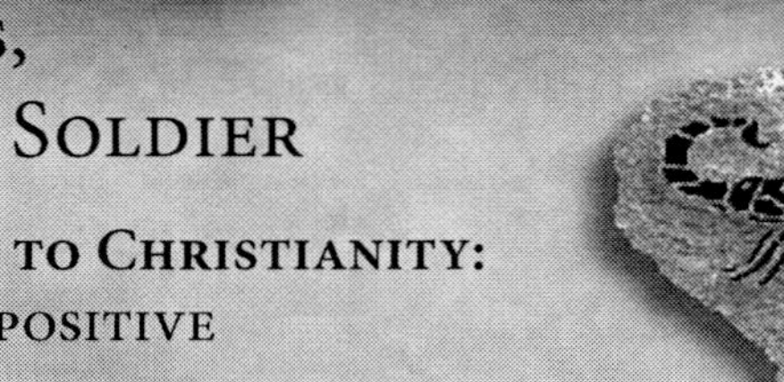

Openness to Christianity:
Neutral-positive

Description: You are a battle-hardened veteran. You follow orders and don't question your superiors. However, you have seen these Christians and you know that they are not criminals. This bothers you although you haven't said anything to anyone. There is something about Paul and his message that you find attractive, although you struggle to explain it to others. To become a Christian means deserting the army. If they catch you it would mean certain execution. You can convert if you like but remember what that would mean.

Cestus, Roman Soldier

Openness to Christianity: Neutral-positive

Description: You are a battle-hardened veteran. You follow orders and don't question your superiors. However, you have seen these Christians and you know that they are not criminals. This bothers you although you haven't said anything to anyone. There is something about Paul and his message that you find attractive, although you struggle to explain it to others. To become a Christian means deserting the army. If they catch you it would mean certain execution. You can convert if you like but remember what that would mean.

Processus, Roman Soldier (assistant to Quartus, the jailor)

Openness to Christianity:
Neutral-positive

Description: You are a battle-hardened veteran. You follow orders and don't question your superiors. However, you have seen these Christians and you know that they are not criminals. This bothers you although you haven't said anything to anyone. To become a Christian means deserting the army. If they catch you it would mean certain execution. You can convert if you like but remember what that would mean.

Martinianus, Roman Soldier (assistant to Quartus, the jailor)

Openness to Christianity:
Neutral-positive

Description: You are a battle-hardened veteran. You follow orders and don't question your superiors. However, you have seen these Christians and you know that they are not criminals. This bothers you although you haven't said anything to anyone. To become a Christian means deserting the army. If they catch you it would mean certain execution. You can convert if you like—but only Peter, by a direct and personal appeal, will be able to convert you.

Roman Citizen (informant)

Openness to Christianity:
Falsely open; 100% loyal to Rome (Nero)

Description: When you hear Peter's message willingly convert. At some point you must betray your church by leading the Roman soldiers to their hiding place. Be sly. Try to do this without revealing that you are really an informant. Here are some ideas: 1) When Peter asks for a courier to deliver Christian documents volunteer, then find the soldiers and lead them to your church and 2) During the day phase try to tip off the soldiers about possible hiding places and/ or any other information you think is important.

Roman Citizen (informant)

Openness to Christianity:
Falsely open; 100% loyal to Rome (Nero)

Description: When you hear Paul's message willingly convert. At some point you must betray your church by leading the Roman soldiers to their hiding place. Be sly. Try to do this without revealing that you are really an informant. Here are some ideas: 1) When Paul asks for a courier to deliver Christian documents volunteer, then find the soldiers and lead them to your church and 2) During the day phase try to tip off the soldiers about possible hiding places and/ or any other information you think is important.

Roman Citizen (informant)

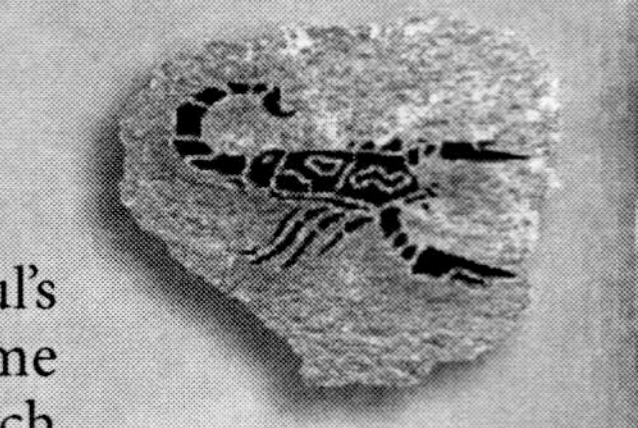

Openness to Christianity:
Falsely open; 100% loyal to Rome (Nero)

Description: When you hear Paul's message willingly convert. At some point you must betray your church by leading the Roman soldiers to their hiding place. Be sly. Try to do this without revealing that you are really an informant. Here are some ideas: 1) When Paul asks for a courier to deliver Christian documents volunteer, then find the soldiers and lead them to your church and 2) During the day phase try to tip off the soldiers about possible hiding places and/ or any other information you think is important.

Quartus

Openness to Christianity:
Neutral

Description: You are the Roman jailor. This is a position of great responsibility. The Emperor himself has entrusted you with the care of his prisoners. Some will be crucified, others will be held for a time and eventually set free. You are curious about Christianity. You see quite clearly that the Christians you hold in your jail are hardly guilty of 'hatred of humanity' or, for that matter, any other crime. However, conversion is very risky. Nero is not one to be trifled with. If you do convert, conduct yourself with due care. You might be more help to the Church alive than dead.

Executioner

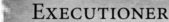

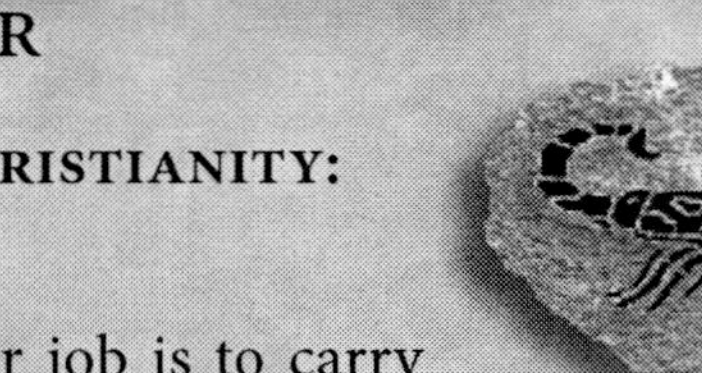

Openness to Christianity:
None

Description: Your job is to carry out the orders of the Emperor. See that each martyr that is condemned to death is tied to their cross. Make sure that the makeup used to write on the martyrs' faces is readily available. Collect the crosses and makeup after each execution.

Executioner

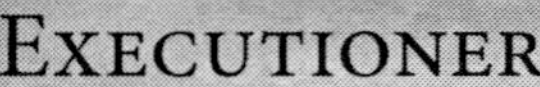

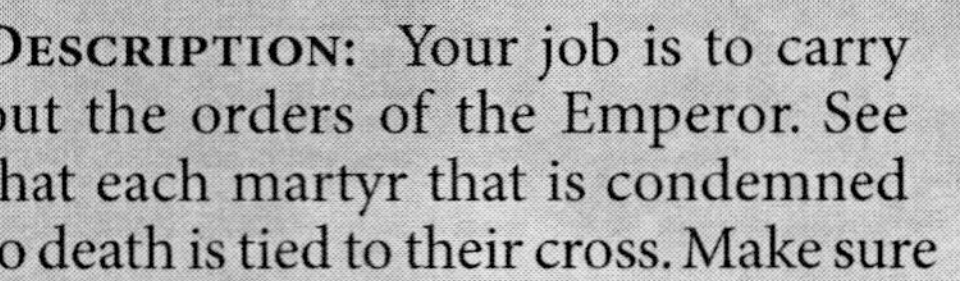

Openness to Christianity:
Neutral

Description: Your job is to carry out the orders of the Emperor. See that each martyr that is condemned to death is tied to their cross. Make sure that the makeup used to write on the martyrs' faces is readily available. Collect the crosses and makeup after each execution. In your case, conversion is an option but remember that you will be executed if caught—probably without a trial.

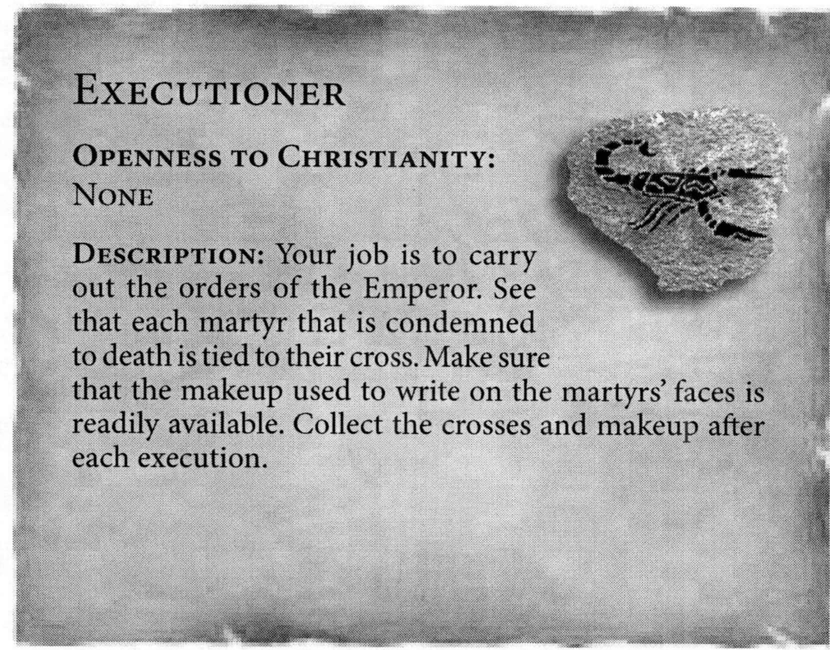

Executioner

Openness to Christianity:
None

Description: Your job is to carry out the orders of the Emperor. See that each martyr that is condemned to death is tied to their cross. Make sure that the makeup used to write on the martyrs' faces is readily available. Collect the crosses and makeup after each execution.

Roman Citizen

Openness to Christianity:
Neutral

Description: You are a poor citizen. Your life is work, work, work and hunger. Deep down you wonder if this is all there is in life. You hope it isn't. You want to believe that there is more out there than the selfish and untrustworthy Roman gods and goddesses. Ask Paul to tell you about his God. If he speaks about love and forgiveness—you convert. If not, then try Peter.

Roman Citizen

Openness to Christianity:
Neutral

Description: You are a poor citizen. Your life is work, work, work and hunger. Deep down you wonder if this is all there is in life. You hope it isn't. You want to believe that there is more out there than the selfish and untrustworthy Roman gods and goddesses. Ask Peter to tell you about his God. If he speaks about love and forgiveness—you convert. If not, then you can laugh at him and reject his God.

Roman Citizen

Openness to Christianity:
Hostile

Description: You are a small shop-owner. You make your money by selling meat that has been used in temple sacrifices to the gods and goddesses. Christianity has no sacrifices and denies the very existence of other gods. This could really hurt your business. If you convert, you are going to have to be deeply and emotionally moved by what Peter and Paul say.

Roman Citizen

Openness to Christianity:
Neutral

Description: You are a baker. Business has been up and down. However, at least you have enough to eat and your children are well-fed. What does Christianity have to offer you? How will it make your life better? You will have to be convinced. Make Peter or Paul answer your questions.

Roman Citizen

Openness to Christianity:
Open

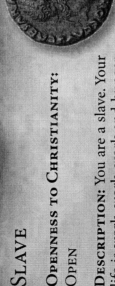

Description: You are a poor citizen. Your life is work, work, work and hunger. Deep down you wonder if this is all there is in life. You hope it isn't. You are a very committed person and a natural leader. If you convert do everything in your power to help Peter or Paul expand the Church.

Slave

Openness to Christianity:
Open

Description: You are a slave. Your life is work, work, work and hunger.
You are the property of one of the senators—you can choose which one. Deep down you wonder if this is all there is in life. You hope it isn't. Christianity's message of equality and freedom appeal to you but you will have to be very careful. If your master (the senator) converts, you can convert. However, if the senator does not, you will have to be an "undercover Christian." As a slave you cannot leave your master without permission so actually staying with the Church is impossible. The best you can do is willingly hear the apostles preach.

Slave

Openness to Christianity:
Open

Description: You are a slave. Your life is work, work, work and hunger.
You are the property of one of the senators—you can choose which one. Deep down you wonder if this is all there is in life. You hope it isn't. Christianity's message of equality and freedom appeal to you but you will have to be very careful. If your master (the senator) converts, you can convert. However, if the senator does not, you will have to be an "undercover Christian." As a slave you cannot leave your master without permission so actually staying with the Church is impossible. The best you can do is willingly hear the apostles preach.

Slave

Openness to Christianity:
Neutral

Description: You are a slave. Your life is work, work, work and hunger.
You are the property of Nero's wife, Poppaea. Christianity's message of equality and freedom appeal to you but you will have to be very careful. If you convert you will have to run away from Nero. If you are caught there will be no mercy—you will be cruelly tortured. If you do choose to convert, you may have to remain with Poppaea. If you stay with her—try to convert her to Christianity. Her power and influence with Nero could result in Christians being saved. You are the only chance the churches have to convert her.

Roman Citizen

Openness to Christianity:
Neutral

Description: You are a poor citizen. Your life is work, work, work and hunger. Deep down you wonder if this is all there is in life. You hope it isn't. You start out by making fun of Peter. To you, he is nothing more than what you are—poor, uneducated and powerless. If Peter takes the time to personally reach out to you, you are moved by his love. Tell him you will think it over (wait one turn). On the next day phase, talk to Peter. If he impresses you again convert.

Roman Citizen

Openness to Christianity:
Hostile

Description: You are a small shop-owner. You make your money by selling meat that has been used in temple sacrifices to the gods and goddesses. Christianity has no sacrifices and denies the very existence of other gods. This could really hurt your business. If you convert, you are going to have to be deeply and emotionally moved by what Peter and Paul say.

Roman Citizen

Openness to Christianity:
Neutral

Description: You are a blacksmith. Business has been up and down. However, at least you have enough to eat and your children are well-fed. What does Christianity have to offer you? How will it make your life better? You will have to be convinced. Make Peter or Paul answer your questions.

Roman Citizen

Openness to Christianity:
Open

Description: You are a poor citizen. Your life is work, work, work and hunger. Deep down you wonder if this is all there is in life. You hope it isn't. You are a very committed person and a natural leader. If you convert do everything in your power to help Paul expand the Church.

Seneca, Roman Citizen

Openness to Christianity:
Neutral

Description: You are a philosopher and teacher in the Rhetor (university). You are well educated and somewhat snotty. However, as a philosopher you are always interested in new ideas. Engage the apostles in discussion and debate. Remember, you are more educated than Peter and at least as educated as Paul (probably more). What does Christianity have to offer you? How will it make your life better? You will have to be convinced. Make Peter or Paul answer your questions. Be tough on them.

Quintus, Roman Citizen

Openness to Christianity:
Hostile

Description: You are a philosopher and teacher in the Rhetor (university). You are well educated and somewhat snotty. As a philosopher you are always interested in new ideas but not so much because you really care about them but because they are new and it is your business to be familiar with new ideas. Engage the apostles in discussion and debate. Remember, you are more educated than Peter and at least as educated as Paul (probably more). Make Peter or Paul answer your questions. Be tough on them.

Patroclus, Slave

Openness to Christianity:
Neutral-positive

Description: You are a slave. Your life is work, work, work and hunger. You are the property of Nero. Christianity's message of equality and freedom appeal to you but you will have to be very careful. You find yourself drawn to Paul and his message. If you convert you will have to run away from Nero. If you are caught there will be no mercy, you will be cruelly tortured.

Roman Citizen

Openness to Christianity:
Neutral

Description: You are a poor citizen. Your life is work, work, work and hunger. Deep down you wonder if this is all there is in life. You hope it isn't. You start out by making fun of Paul. To you, he is nothing more than what you are—poor, uneducated and powerless. If Paul takes the time to personally reach out to you, you are moved by his love. Tell him you will think it over (wait one turn). On the next day phase, talk to Paul. If he impresses you again—convert.

Roman Citizen

Openness to Christianity:
Hostile

Description: You are a priest of Jupiter. You make your money by temple sacrifices to the Great God Jupiter. Christianity has no sacrifices and denies the very existence of other gods. This could really hurt your business. These Christians will have to be stopped. After all the old Roman religions are traditional and this "new" religion is trying to crowd your turf.

Roman Citizen

Openness to Christianity:
Neutral

Description: You are a leather worker. Business has been up and down. However, at least you have enough to eat and your children are well-fed. What does Christianity have to offer you? How will it make your life better? You will have to be convinced. Make Peter or Paul answer your questions.

Roman Citizen

Openness to Christianity:
Open

Description: You are poor. Your life is work, work, work and hunger. Deep down you wonder if this is all there is in life. You hope it isn't. You are a very committed person and a natural leader. If you convert do everything in your power to help Peter expand the Church.

Roman Citizen

Openness to Christianity:
Neutral

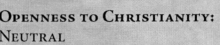

Description: You are a priest of Bacchus. You make your money by temple banquets and drunken orgies. Christianity has no sacrifices and denies the very existence of other gods. Deep down you don't believe in Bacchus—he is just an excuse for people to party. Something inside you is asking for more. Listen to the apostles. Could this be what you are looking for?

Candida

Openness to Christianity:
Positive-Neutral

Description: You are the wife of Quartus who is the Roman jailor. You are attracted to Paul's preaching and are likely to convert to Christianity, assuming that Paul is an effective preacher. If you choose to convert, your first job is to try to convert your husband. Introduce him to Paul. Having influence with the jailor will be of great significance to the Christians. It will allow them access to their people who are martyrs for the faith (both those that are condemned to die and those who are to serve temporary jail terms).

Roman Citizen

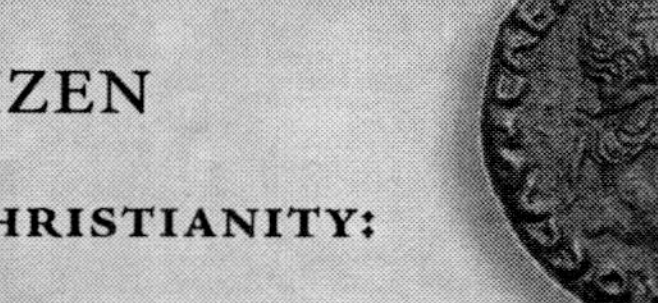

Openness to Christianity:
Neutral

Description: You are the operator of the Roman tavern. (Ask the gamemaster for details.) Business has been good. You have plenty of possessions. You have wealth. Why do you feel so pathetic? What does Christianity have to offer you? How will it make your life better? You will have to be convinced. Make Peter or Paul answer your questions.

Simon Magus

Openness to Christianity:
None

Description: You are a magician and a trickster. You want to gain followers to your way of thinking. *You will be the main competition for Peter and Paul (religiously speaking).* You must try to gain followers to your religion. Your beliefs:

1) You are the power of God himself—God in the flesh.

2) You have been sent to this world to reveal the truth to people. The truth that you preach is that people are not really what and who they think they are. They are really gods, exiled into this world. They have forgotten who they really are and are in deep need of being told that they come from God and must return to God.

You have great powers. Tell stories of the great things you have done: flying, killing people with a mere word, raising the dead, healing people, etc.

Agrippina

Openness to Christianity:
Neutral-Positive

Description: You are a female concubine (a woman who lives with a man without being married to him; a secondary wife) of Agrippa. You follow Agrippa wherever he goes. He is your master. However, you are becoming more and more restless. You are searching for meaning in your life. When you hear the preaching of Peter, it stirs you in a powerful way. The choice is yours—Agrippa or the man this Peter calls Jesus.

Nicaria

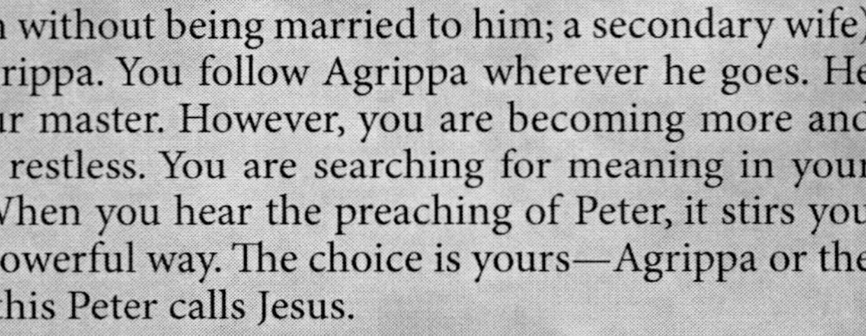

Openness to Christianity:
Neutral-Positive

Description: You are a female concubine (a woman who lives with a man without being married to him; a secondary wife) of Agrippa. You follow Agrippa wherever he goes. He is your master. However, you are becoming more and more restless. You are searching for meaning in your life. When you hear the preaching of Peter, it stirs you in a powerful way. The choice is yours—Agrippa or the man this Peter calls Jesus.

Doris

Openness to Christianity:
Neutral-Positive

Description: You are a female concubine (a woman who lives with a man without being married to him; a secondary wife) of Agrippa. You follow Agrippa wherever he goes. He is your master. However, you are becoming more and more restless. You are searching for meaning in your life. When you hear the preaching of Peter, it stirs you in a powerful way. The choice is yours—Agrippa or the man this Peter calls Jesus.

Rufina

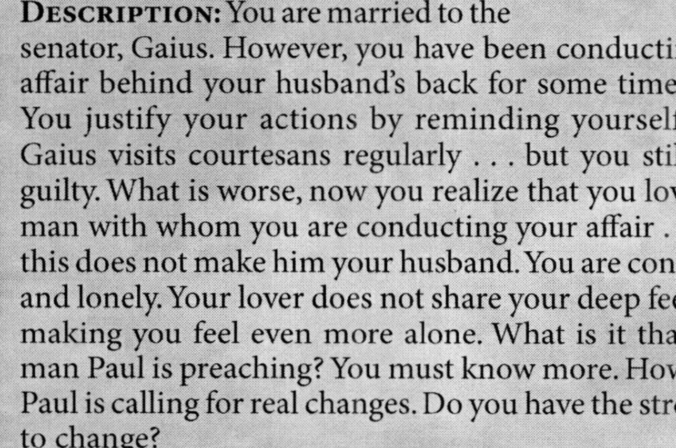

Openness to Christianity:
Neutral

Description: You are married to the senator, Gaius. However, you have been conducting an affair behind your husband's back for some time now. You justify your actions by reminding yourself that Gaius visits courtesans regularly . . . but you still feel guilty. What is worse, now you realize that you love the man with whom you are conducting your affair . . . but this does not make him your husband. You are confused and lonely. Your lover does not share your deep feelings making you feel even more alone. What is it that this man Paul is preaching? You must know more. However, Paul is calling for real changes. Do you have the strength to change?

Euphemia

Openness to Christianity:
Neutral-Positive

Description: You are a female concubine (a woman who lives with a man without being married to him; a secondary wife) of Agrippa. You follow Agrippa wherever he goes. He is your master. However, you are becoming more and more restless. You are searching for meaning in your life. When you hear the preaching of Peter, it stirs you in a powerful way. The choice is yours—Agrippa or the man this Peter calls Jesus.

Xanthippe

Openness to Christianity:
Neutral-Positive

Description: You are the wife of Albinus. You follow Albinus wherever he goes. He is your master. However, you are becoming more and more restless. You are searching for meaning in your life. When you hear the preaching of Peter, it stirs you in a powerful way. The choice is yours—Albinus or the man this Peter calls Jesus.

Slave

Openness to Christianity:
Neutral

Description: You are a slave. Your life is work, work, work. You are the property of the tavern keeper. Christianity's message of equality and freedom appeal to you but you will have to be very careful. If you convert you may have to run away from your master. However, if the tavern keeper is a Christian as well, there may be no need to flee. If you do flee and are caught there will be no mercy—you will be cruelly tortured. You will not be tried in court.

Slave

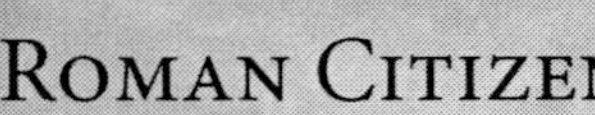

Openness to Christianity:
Neutral

Description: You are a slave. Your life is work, work, work. You are the property of Nero. You are the Emperor's official scribe (secretary). You will be in charge of writing and delivering any letters Nero may need to send. Further, you are the Emperor's message bearer for any verbal communications Nero may care to send. Make sure that you inform the Emperor of your duties so that you can be of service immediately and as needed in the game.

Roman Citizen

Openness to Christianity:
Neutral

Description: You are a poor citizen. Your life is work, work, work and hunger. Deep down you wonder if this is all there is in life. You hope it isn't. You want to believe that there is more out there than the selfish and untrustworthy Roman gods and goddesses. Ask Paul to tell you about his God. If he speaks about love and forgiveness you convert. If not, then try Peter.

Roman Citizen

Openness to Christianity:
Neutral

Description: You are a poor citizen. Your life is work, work, work and hunger. Deep down you wonder if this is all there is in life. You hope it isn't. You want to believe that there is more out there than the selfish and untrustworthy Roman gods and goddesses. Ask Peter to tell you about his God. If he speaks about love and forgiveness you convert. If not, then you can laugh at him and reject his God.

Roman Citizen

Openness to Christianity:
Hostile

Description: You are a small shop-owner. You make your money by selling meat that has been used in temple sacrifices to the gods and goddesses. Christianity has no sacrifices and denies the very existence of other gods. This could really hurt your business. If you convert, you are going to have to be deeply and emotionally moved by what Peter and Paul say.

Roman Citizen

Openness to Christianity:
Neutral

Description: You are a baker. Business has been up and down. However, at least you have enough to eat and your children are well-fed. What does Christianity have to offer you? How will it make your life better? You will have to be convinced. Make Peter or Paul answer your questions.

Roman Citizen

Openness to Christianity:
Open

Description: You are a poor citizen. Your life is work, work, work and hunger. Deep down you wonder if this is all there is in life. You hope it isn't. You are a very committed person and a natural leader. If you convert do everything in your power to help Peter or Paul expand the Church.

Roman Citizen

Openness to Christianity:
Neutral

Description: You are a poor citizen. Your life is work, work, work and hunger. Deep down you wonder if this is all there is in life. You hope it isn't. You want to believe that there is more out there than the selfish and untrustworthy Roman gods and goddesses. Ask Paul to tell you about his God. If he speaks about love and forgiveness you convert. If not, then try Peter.

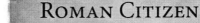

Gemellus, Roman Citizen

Openness to Christianity:
Neutral-Negative

Description: You are a wealthy citizen. You are an ardent supporter of Simon Magus. Support Simon's activities and quickly become his disciple. It is your intention to prove to everyone that Simon is, in fact, who he says he is—the very Power of God. Listen closely to Simon's claims, then help him "preach" to the people of Rome. Help Simon form a group of supporters. Once you are strong enough, start to attack the Christians by speaking out against them, spreading bad rumors about the Church and generally being argumentative with their leaders.

Roman Citizen

Openness to Christianity:
Neutral

Description: You are a poor citizen.
Your life is work, work, work and hunger. Deep down you wonder if this is all there is in life. You hope it isn't. You want to believe that there is more out there than the selfish and untrustworthy Roman gods and goddesses. Ask Peter to tell you about his God. If he speaks about love and forgiveness you convert. If not, then you can laugh at him and reject his God.

Roman Citizen

Openness to Christianity:
Hostile

Description: You are a small shop-owner. You make your money by selling meat that has been used in temple sacrifices to the gods and goddesses. Christianity has no sacrifices and denies the very existence of other gods. This could really hurt your business. If you convert, you are going to have to be deeply and emotionally moved by what Peter and Paul say.

Roman Citizen

Openness to Christianity:
Neutral

Description: You are a baker.
Business has been up and down. However, at least you have enough to eat and your children are well-fed. What does Christianity have to offer you? How will it make your life better? You will have to be convinced. Make Peter or Paul answer your questions.

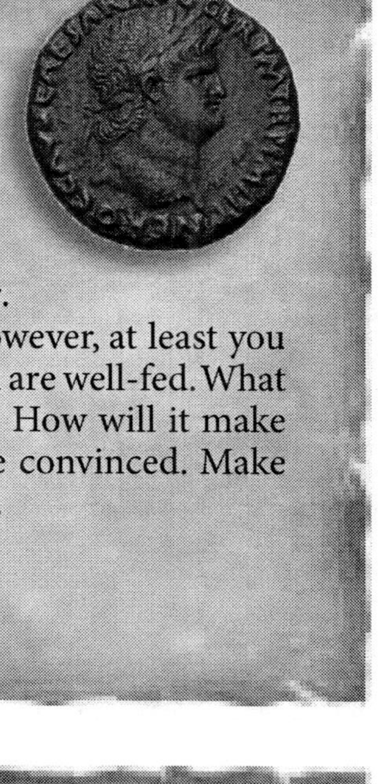

Roman Citizen

Openness to Christianity:
Open

Description: You are a poor citizen.
Your life is work, work, work and hunger. Deep down you wonder if this is all there is in life. You hope it isn't. You are a very committed person and a natural leader. If you convert do everything in your power to help Peter or Paul expand the Church.

Roman Citizen

Openness to Christianity:
Neutral

Description: You are a poor citizen.
Your life is work, work, work and hunger. Deep down you wonder if this is all there is in life. You hope it isn't. You want to believe that there is more out there than the selfish and untrustworthy Roman gods and goddesses. Ask Paul to tell you about his God. If he speaks about love and forgiveness you convert. If not, then try Peter.

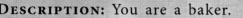

Roman Citizen

Openness to Christianity:
Neutral

Description: You are a poor citizen.
Your life is work, work, work and hunger. Deep down you wonder if this is all there is in life. You hope it isn't. You want to believe that there is more out there than the selfish and untrustworthy Roman gods and goddesses. Ask Peter to tell you about his God. If he speaks about love and forgiveness you convert. If not, then you can laugh at him and reject his God.

Roman Citizen

Openness to Christianity:
Hostile

Description: You are a small shop-owner. You make your money by selling meat that has been used in temple sacrifices to the gods and goddesses. Christianity has no sacrifices and denies the very existence of other gods. This could really hurt your business. If you convert, you are going to have to be deeply and emotionally moved by what Peter and Paul say.

Roman Citizen

Openness to Christianity:
Neutral

Description: You are a baker. Business has been up and down. However, at least you have enough to eat and your children are well-fed. What does Christianity have to offer you? How will it make your life better? You will have to be convinced. Make Peter or Paul answer your questions.

Roman Citizen

Openness to Christianity:
Open

Description: You are a poor citizen. Your life is work, work, work and hunger. Deep down you wonder if this is all there is in life. You hope it isn't. You are a very committed person and a natural leader. If you convert do everything in your power to help Peter or Paul expand the Church.

Roman Citizen

Openness to Christianity:
Neutral

Description: You are a poor citizen. Your life is work, work, work and hunger. Deep down you wonder if this is all there is in life. You hope it isn't. You want to believe that there is more out there than the selfish and untrustworthy Roman gods and goddesses. Ask Paul to tell you about his God. If he speaks about love and forgiveness you convert. If not, then try Peter.

Roman Citizen

Openness to Christianity:
Neutral

Description: You are a poor citizen. Your life is work, work, work and hunger. Deep down you wonder if this is all there is in life. You hope it isn't. You want to believe that there is more out there than the selfish and untrustworthy Roman gods and goddesses. Ask Peter to tell you about his God. If he speaks about love and forgiveness you convert. If not, then you can laugh at him and reject his God.

Roman Citizen

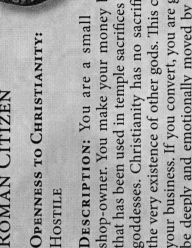

Openness to Christianity:
Hostile

Description: You are a small shop-owner. You make your money by selling meat that has been used in temple sacrifices to the gods and goddesses. Christianity has no sacrifices and denies the very existence of other gods. This could really hurt your business. If you convert, you are going to have to be deeply and emotionally moved by what Peter and Paul say.

Roman Citizen

Openness to Christianity:
Neutral

Description: You are a baker. Business has been up and down. However, at least you have enough to eat and your children are well-fed. What does Christianity have to offer you? How will it make your life better? You will have to be convinced. Make Peter or Paul answer your questions.

Roman Citizen

Openness to Christianity:
Open

Description: You are a poor citizen. Your life is work, work, work and hunger. Deep down you wonder if this is all there is in life. You hope it isn't. You are a very committed person and a natural leader. If you convert do everything in your power to help Peter or Paul expand the Church.

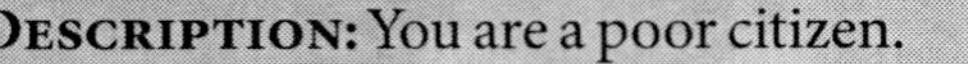

Roman Citizen

Openness to Christianity:
Neutral

Description: You are a poor citizen.
Your life is work, work, work and hunger. Deep down you wonder if this is all there is in life. You hope it isn't. You want to believe that there is more out there than the selfish and untrustworthy Roman gods and goddesses. Ask Peter to tell you about his God. If he speaks about love and forgiveness you convert. If not, then you can laugh at him and reject his God.

Roman Citizen

Openness to Christianity:
Hostile

Description: You are a small shop-owner. You make your money by selling meat that has been used in temple sacrifices to the gods and goddesses. Christianity has no sacrifices and denies the very existence of other gods. This could really hurt your business. If you convert, you are going to have to be deeply and emotionally moved by what Peter and Paul say.

Roman Citizen

Openness to Christianity:
Neutral

Description: You are a baker.
Business has been up and down. However, at least you have enough to eat and your children are well-fed. What does Christianity have to offer you? How will it make your life better? You will have to be convinced. Make Peter or Paul answer your questions.

Roman Citizen

Openness to Christianity:
Open

Description: You are a poor citizen.
Your life is work, work, work and hunger. Deep down you wonder if this is all there is in life. You hope it isn't. You are a very committed person and a natural leader. If you convert do everything in your power to help Peter or Paul expand the Church.

Slave

Openness to Christianity:
Open

Description: You are a slave. Your life is work, work, work and hunger. You are the property of one of the senators—you can choose which one. Deep down you wonder if this is all there is in life. You hope it isn't. Christianity's message of equality and freedom appeal to you but you will have to be very careful. If your master (the senator) converts, you can convert. However, if the senator does not, you will have to be an "undercover Christian." As a slave you cannot leave your master without permission so actually staying with the Church is impossible. The best you can do is willingly hear the apostles preach.

Slave

Openness to Christianity:
Open

Description: You are a slave. Your life is work, work, work and hunger. You are the property of one of the senators—you can choose which one. Deep down you wonder if this is all there is in life. You hope it isn't. Christianity's message of equality and freedom appeal to you but you will have to be very careful. If your master (the senator) converts, you can convert. However, if the senator does not, you will have to be an "undercover Christian." As a slave you cannot leave your master without permission so actually staying with the Church is impossible. The best you can do is willingly hear the apostles preach.

Slave

Openness to Christianity:
Open

Description: You are a slave. Your life is work, work, work and hunger. You are the property of one of the senators—you can choose which one. Deep down you wonder if this is all there is in life. You hope it isn't. Christianity's message of equality and freedom appeal to you but you will have to be very careful. If your master (the senator) converts, you can convert. However, if the senator does not, you will have to be an "undercover Christian." As a slave you cannot leave your master without permission so actually staying with the Church is impossible. The best you can do is willingly hear the apostles preach.

Slave

Openness to Christianity:
Open

Description: You are a slave. Your life is work, work, work and hunger. You are the property of one of the senators—you can choose which one. Deep down you wonder if this is all there is in life. You hope it isn't. Christianity's message of equality and freedom appeal to you but you will have to be very careful. If your master (the senator) converts, you can convert. However, if the senator does not, you will have to be an "undercover Christian." As a slave you cannot leave your master without permission so actually staying with the Church is impossible. The best you can do is willingly hear the apostles preach.

Slave

Openness to Christianity:
Open

Description: You are a slave. Your life is work, work, work and hunger. You are the property of one of the senators—you can choose which one. Deep down you wonder if this is all there is in life. You hope it isn't. Christianity's message of equality and freedom appeal to you but you will have to be very careful. If your master (the senator) converts, you can convert. However, if the senator does not, you will have to be an "undercover Christian." As a slave you cannot leave your master without permission so actually staying with the Church is impossible. The best you can do is willingly hear the apostles preach.

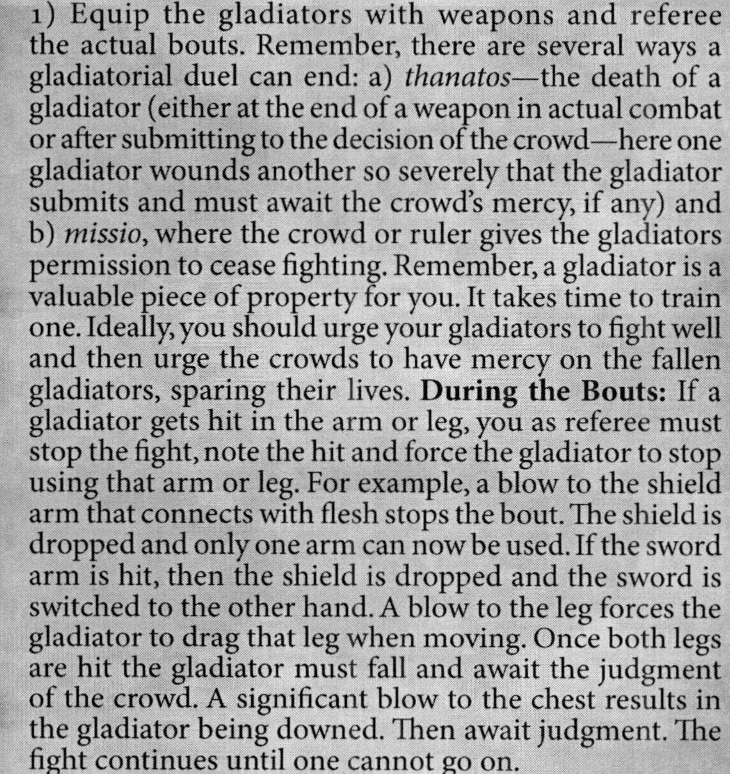

Viterbius, the Lanista

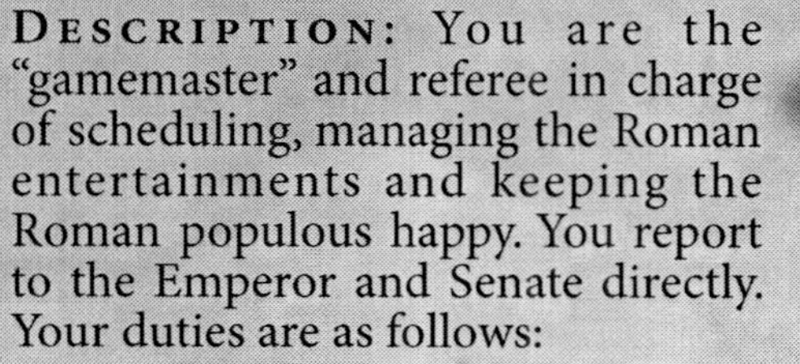

Openness to Christianity:
Neutral

Description: You are the "gamemaster" and referee in charge of scheduling, managing the Roman entertainments and keeping the Roman populous happy. You report to the Emperor and Senate directly. Your duties are as follows:

1) Equip the gladiators with weapons and referee the actual bouts. Remember, there are several ways a gladiatorial duel can end: a) *thanatos*—the death of a gladiator (either at the end of a weapon in actual combat or after submitting to the decision of the crowd—here one gladiator wounds another so severely that the gladiator submits and must await the crowd's mercy, if any) and b) *missio*, where the crowd or ruler gives the gladiators permission to cease fighting. Remember, a gladiator is a valuable piece of property for you. It takes time to train one. Ideally, you should urge your gladiators to fight well and then urge the crowds to have mercy on the fallen gladiators, sparing their lives. **During the Bouts:** If a gladiator gets hit in the arm or leg, you as referee must stop the fight, note the hit and force the gladiator to stop using that arm or leg. For example, a blow to the shield arm that connects with flesh stops the bout. The shield is dropped and only one arm can now be used. If the sword arm is hit, then the shield is dropped and the sword is switched to the other hand. A blow to the leg forces the gladiator to drag that leg when moving. Once both legs are hit the gladiator must fall and await the judgment of the crowd. A significant blow to the chest results in the gladiator being downed. Then await judgment. The fight continues until one cannot go on.

2) Referee the boxing matches. Each round should be 30 seconds (timed). After the end of each round, ask the Senate to vote on who won the round. The winner of the match must win 2 of 3 rounds.

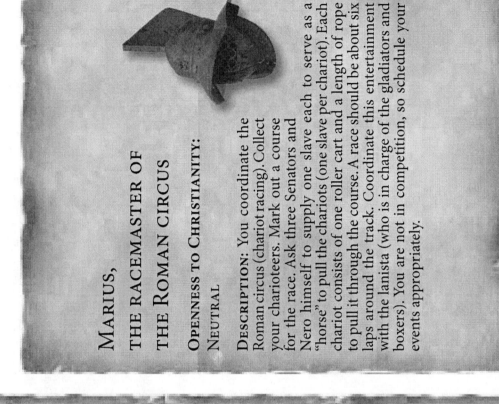

Marius, the Racemaster of the Roman Circus

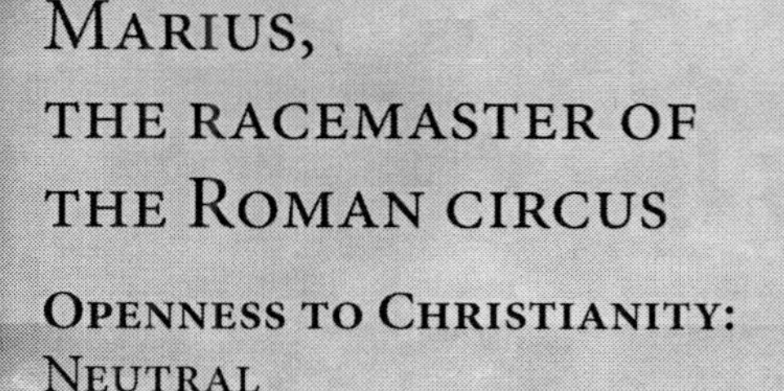

Openness to Christianity:
Neutral

Description: You coordinate the Roman circus (chariot racing). Collect your charioteers. Mark out a course for the race. Ask three Senators and Nero himself to supply one slave each to serve as a "horse" to pull the chariots (one slave per chariot). Each chariot consists of one roller cart and a length of rope to pull it through the course. A race should be about six laps around the track. Coordinate this entertainment with the lanista (who is in charge of the gladiators and boxers). You are not in competition, so schedule your events appropriately.

Charioteer

Openness to Christianity:
Neutral

Description: You are a professional athlete, equivalent to a modern race car driver. Your work is extremely dangerous—you could literally die during any race. However, the bright side of this is that you are extremely popular with the ladies and, if you win, there is the potential for great riches. You are to report to the racemaster who is in charge of the Roman circus. He will work with the lanista to schedule the order of events (chariot racing, boxing, gladiatorial bouts). Follow his instructions.

Charioteer

Openness to Christianity:
Neutral

Description: You are a professional athlete, equivalent to a modern race car driver. Your work is extremely dangerous—you could literally die during any race. However, the bright side of this is that you are extremely popular with the ladies and, if you win, there is the potential for great riches. You are to report to the racemaster who is in charge of the Roman circus. He will work with the lanista to schedule the order of events (chariot racing, boxing, gladiatorial bouts). Follow his instructions.

Charioteer

Openness to Christianity:
Neutral

Description: You are a professional athlete, equivalent to a modern race car driver. Your work is extremely dangerous—you could literally die during any race. However, the bright side of this is that you are extremely popular with the ladies and, if you win, there is the potential for great riches. You are to report to the racemaster who is in charge of the Roman circus. He will work with the lanista to schedule the order of events (chariot racing, boxing, gladiatorial bouts). Follow his instructions.

Charioteer

Openness to Christianity:
Neutral

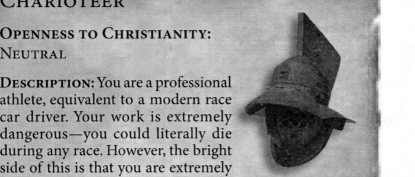

Description: You are a professional athlete, equivalent to a modern race car driver. Your work is extremely dangerous—you could literally die during any race. However, the bright side of this is that you are extremely popular with the ladies and, if you win, there is the potential for great riches. You are to report to the racemaster who is in charge of the Roman circus. He will work with the lanista to schedule the order of events (chariot racing, boxing, gladiatorial bouts). Follow his instructions.

Gladiator

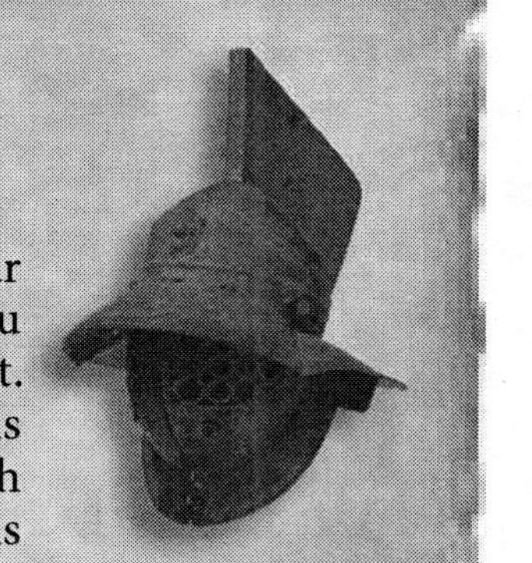

Openness to Christianity:
Neutral

Description: You are a slave. Your work is extremely dangerous—you could literally die during any fight. However, the bright side of this is that you are extremely popular with the ladies and, if you win, there is the potential for great riches. You are to report to the lanista who is in charge of the Roman entertainment. He will schedule the order of events (boxing, gladiatorial bouts). Follow his instructions.

Gladiator

Openness to Christianity:
Neutral

Description: You are a slave. Your work is extremely dangerous—you could literally die during any fight. However, the bright side of this is that you are extremely popular with the ladies and, if you win, there is the potential for great riches. You are to report to the lanista who is in charge of the Roman entertainment. He will schedule the order of events (boxing, gladiatorial bouts). Follow his instructions.

Boxer

Openness to Christianity:
Neutral

Description: You are an athlete. You are extremely popular with the ladies and, if you win, there is the potential for great riches. You are to report to the lanista who is in charge of the Roman entertainment. He will schedule the order of events (boxing, gladiatorial bouts). Follow his instructions.

Boxer

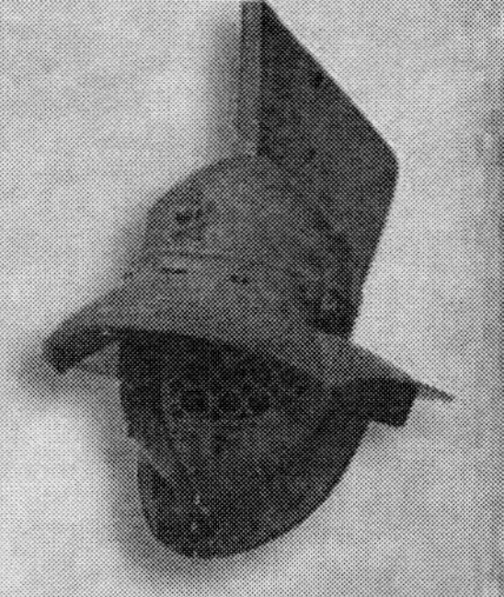

Openness to Christianity:
Neutral

Description: You are an athlete. You are extremely popular with the ladies and, if you win, there is the potential for great riches. You are to report to the lanista who is in charge of the Roman entertainment. He will schedule the order of events (boxing, gladiatorial bouts). Follow his instructions.

Introduction and Historical Overview of Martyrdom and Persecution in the Early Church

A Crash Course for Youth Ministers, Campus Ministers, and Church History Instructors

Persecution and martyrdom have always been a part of the lived experience of the Church. The following essay is intended to elucidate some of the basic issues that are related to a study of martyrdom and persecution in the early Church. While it shall be my practice to employ direct quotations from the ancient sources (as opposed to more general statements) whenever possible, this discussion is intended to be introductory in character.

Part 1
Ominous Beginnings

In AD 30, Jesus of Nazareth was crucified at the hands of the Roman Prefect Pontius Pilate. This fact is well-known but rarely does the ordinary Christian reflect on the significance of this act for the early Christians who would later attempt to preach his message to the Greco-Roman world.

Crucifixion was a particularly nasty way to die. The Roman statesman and orator, Cicero (106–43 BC) calls it "that most cruel and disgusting penalty" (*Verr.* 2.5.165). Josephus, the first century Jewish historian, calls crucifixion "the most wretched of deaths" (*JW* 7.203). It often involved scourging beforehand (as was the case with Jesus; Mark 15:15) but *not* beating with rods (contra Mel Gibson's movie, *The Passion of the Christ*). The Romans used the *flagellum* typically—although not exclusively—for slaves and provincials. Rods were normally used for free citizens. After this beating, the victims were forced to carry either a crossbeam or the entire cross to the place of execution, which was inevitably a public location. The Roman rhetorician, Quintillian (ca. AD 35–95) explains why this was the Roman practice: "Whenever we crucify the guilty, the most crowded roads are chosen, where the most people can see and be moved by this fear. For penalties relate not so much to retribution as to their exemplary effect" (*Decl.* 274). The victims were then stripped. They were attached to the crossbeam with ropes or nails, then raised up into the air and seated on a *sedile* or small wooden peg in the upright beam. Ropes were used to bind the shoulders or torso to the cross and the victim's heels were either nailed or tied to the vertical piece. Crucifixion was intended to protract the victim's sufferings and could last for days.

There was apparently no one approved way to crucify a person. The Roman philosopher, Seneca (ca. 4 BC—AD 65), describes the various types of crucifixions: "I see crosses there, not just of one kind but made in many different ways: some have their victims with head down to the ground; some impale their private parts; others stretch out their arms on the gibbet" (*Dial.* 6 [*Cons. Marc.*] 20.3). Josephus affirms this reality in the course of his description of the Roman treatment of the Jews during the siege of Jerusalem: "The soldiers themselves through rage and bitterness nailed up their victims in different postures as a grim joke, till owing to the vast numbers there was no room for the crosses and no crosses for the bodies" (*JW* 5.451).

Among the ancients, no one provides a better sense of the ghastly character of this form of execution than Seneca. In *Epistle* 101, he argues that suicide is to be preferred over crucifixion. His gruesome description of this type of execution proves his point quite convincingly:

> Can anyone be found who would prefer wasting away in pain dying limb by limb, or letting out his life drop by drop, rather than expiring once and for all? Can any man be found willing to be fastened to the accursed tree, long sickly, already deformed, swelling with ugly welts on shoulders and chest, and drawing the breath of life amid long-drawn-out agony? He would have many excuses for dying even before mounting the cross.

Crucifixion was a death that was usually reserved for slaves and non-citizens (although there were exceptions to this norm; see Josephus, *JW* 2.308). The Romans called it the *servile supplicium* (the slaves' punishment). In addition, crucifixion was a type of death typically associated in the popular mind with criminals. This reality is clearly reflected in many ancient sources. For example, the Greek biographer and philosopher, Plutarch (ca. AD 46–120) remarks, "every criminal condemned to death bears his cross on his back" (*Mor.* 554 A/B).

Figure 22

The fact that the founder of Christianity died as a criminal was clearly an impediment to the spread of the Gospel (**see Figure 22**). Around AD 55, when Paul wrote 1 Corinthians, he stated how much the cross had a negative impact on people's perception of the Christian message: ". . . we proclaim Christ crucified, a stumbling block to Jews and foolishness to Gentiles . . ." (1:23). Later, the second century Christian philosopher and apologist Justin echoed Paul's expression of the difficulties the cross presented to the larger secular society of his day, explaining, "... they proclaim our madness to consist in this, that we give to a crucified man a place second to the unchangeable and eternal God, the Creator of all . . ." (*1 Apology* 13). Celsus, the second century Greek philosopher and critic of Christianity, says the very same thing in his attack on Christianity, *On True Doctrine*. His text is now extant only in the biblical theologian Origen's monumental response, *Against Celsus*, written almost a century after Celsus (ca. 248). In his scathing critique Celsus ridicules the Christian allegiance to a crucified man, asking sarcastically if all other executed persons will likewise be considered divine:

> If, after inventing defenses which are absurd, and by which you were ridiculously deluded, you imagine that you really made a good defense, what prevents you from regarding those other individuals who have been condemned, and have died a miserable death, as greater and more divine messengers of heaven? (*Against Celsus* 2.44)

In addition to Jesus dying by the means of an execution typically reserved for criminals, the Gospel of Mark claims that Jesus was killed along with those who were associated with political rebellion (Mark 15:27; see also Matthew 27:38 which is dependant on Mark 15:27 as a source text) (**see Figure 23**). If you were to ask the ordinary person "Who were the two men who were crucified with Jesus?" the answer would likely be "Two thieves." This is not really an accurate understanding of the Greek word that appears in the two texts.

At this point it is helpful to understand the differences in two Greek words that can sometimes share fields of meaning: *kleptēs* and *lēstēs*. The Greek word *kleptēs* is best translated "thief" meaning someone who steals, using subterfuge, secrecy and sometimes, even force. On the other hand, both Mark 15:27 and Matthew 27:38 use plural forms of the word *lēstēs*. Outside and previous to the New Testament *lēstēs* was used to signify any kind of robber (plunderer, highwayman, pirate, etc.) yet always with the implication of the ruthless use of force in seeking the goods of others. In the writings of Josephus, *lēstēs* is strongly associated with Messianic groups and constantly used to describe the Zealots who make armed conflict against Roman rule the content of their life.

FIGURE 23

Certainly, *lēstēs* could be used to make reference to common thieves. However, in light of the political turmoil that simmered in Palestine during the early decades of the first century AD, it seems advisable to think that these "robbers" may have been politically and religiously motivated and closer to the Robin

Hood variety 'bandit' than to a common shoplifter. Therefore, it would seem to be no coincidence that the Romans crucified Jesus, placing a placard above his head that made reference to his assumed aspirations to be "King of the Jews" (i.e., branding Jesus as a political rebel), with two "robbers" who actively opposed Roman rule.

Lending further credence to this interpretation is the fact that the Gospel of Luke, a writing widely understood by scholars to be aimed at a non-Jewish, Greco-Roman audience, removes the word *lēstēs* altogether. Luke replaces *lēstēs* with *kakourgoi*, literally "evildoers." This is part of a general effort on Luke's part to present Jesus as a wrongly-killed victim of mob violence and not a political criminal. In Luke 23, Pilate is presented as thrice declaring Jesus' innocence (23:4, 14 and 22). The centurion echoes this declaration of innocence at the foot of the cross (23:47). Only in the Gospel of Luke is Jesus *not* scourged by the Roman soldiers (Pilate only states that he intends to chastise Jesus, literally to "educate" him; cf. Mark 15:16; Matt 27:27; John 19:2). In the early centuries of Christian history, there was clearly an ongoing need for Christians to disassociate Jesus with banditry. Evidence supporting this assertion is provided by the fact that Celsus calls Jesus a *lēstēs* and on this basis seeks to dismiss him as a false Messiah (*Against Celsus* 2.44).

Certainly it is fair to say that this association with political rebellion was encouraged by some of the terminology used by the early Church. Like their Master, early Christians spoke about the coming "Kingdom of God". Still worse, they referred to Jesus as "Lord" (*kyrios*). In classical Greece *kyrios* was often applied to both gods and human rulers. However, as Roman power grew it began to be more and more associated (although by no means exclusively) with the Roman emperors. As early as the first century BC, *kyrios* was used in Egypt in reference to the Emperor Augustus (12 BC). In addition, evidence exists for its application to the Roman emperor, as a summary of the emperor's position from the time of Claudius (ruled from AD 41–54). In general, *kyrios* seems to have had a steady increase in imperial usage from the time of Nero.

To complicate matters, the Christian writings seem to have a certain, albeit spiritualized, militarism. Imagine how the Letter to the Ephesians' description of a Christian's spiritual armor (6:11–17) might read for a Roman official! How would a Roman governor interpret Ephesians 6:12 (For our struggle is not against enemies of blood and flesh, but against the rulers, against the authorities, against the cosmic powers of this present darkness, against the spiritual forces of evil in the heavenly places)? "What kind of doubletalk is this?" a confused and suspicious Roman might ask. "Is this not an outright admission that Christians intend to struggle against Roman authority?"

Other examples exist. Paul himself in 1Thessalonians 5 uses similar highly charged language that speaks of "sudden destruction" and the "Lord's" advent as a "thief in the night" (recall Celsus' branding of Jesus as a *lēstēs*) from which there will be "no escape" (5:2–3). Several verses later Paul urges Christians to don breastplates and helmets (5:8)! The Book of Revelation, with its thinly veiled references to Rome (as a woman seated on seven hills; 17:9), describes in chapter 19 a great and bloody battle in which the armies of heaven are led by one called "King of Kings and Lord of Lords" who destroys the nations, massacring their armies. If this text fell into Roman hands (as they most assuredly did), such sentiments would not have been read with favor.

An extreme expression of such spiritualized militarism is found in the second century apocryphal *Acts of Paul*. In 11.2, Christians are called "soldiers of Christ" (cf. *Acts of Peter* 36) and described as being in "the army of that king of the ages". Later, when Paul is brought before Nero and has the opportunity to nuance and soften such metaphors, he chooses rather to emphasize these ideas, serving only to infuriate the Emperor Nero. In 11.3, the scene plays out as follows:

> And among the many Paul also was brought bound; to him all his fellow-prisoners gave

> heed, so that Caesar observed that he was the man in command. And he said to him: "Man of the great king, but (now) my prisoner, why did it seem good to you to come secretly into the empire of the Romans and enlist soldiers from my province?" But Paul, filled with the Holy Spirit, said before them all: "Caesar, not only from your province do we enlist soldiers, but from the whole world. For this charge has been laid upon us, that no man be excluded who wishes to serve my king. If you also think it good, do him service! For neither riches nor splendor of this present life will save you, but if you submit and entreat him, then shall you be saved. For in one day he will destroy the world with fire." When Caesar heard this, he commanded all the prisoners to be burned with fire, but Paul to be beheaded according to the law of the Romans.

Needless to say, a certain amount of prudent diplomacy may have been a better course of action. While this text is clearly fictional, such bravado and (one might argue) arrogance in the face of the temporal authorities finds repeated expression in the accounts of the martyrs.

Part 2
The Earliest Clashes with the Authorities

It should be understood clearly that the early communities of Christians did not immediately feel a need or pressure to disassociate themselves with their Jewish roots. All of Jesus' closest followers were Jews and they viewed him as the Jewish Messiah. For many of these early Jewish Christians Jesus represented the logical culmination of God's saving work on behalf of God's people. These Jewish Christians combed the Jewish Scriptures for passages and "prophecies" that helped them interpret and make sense of Jesus' life, ministry and death. This Jewish Christian need to integrate Jesus into a distinctly Jewish religious matrix is captured in New Testament phrases like "in accordance with the Scriptures" (1 Cor 15:3–4) and the many Matthean variants of "this was to fulfill what had been spoken through the prophet . . ." (2:15; 8:17; 12:17; 13:35; etc.).

It should be remembered that first century AD Judaism was a diverse mixture of different sects (e.g., Pharisees, Sadducees, Zealots, the Qumran community, Christians, etc.). We should not imagine that religious differences pitted "the Jews"—as the Gospel of John calls its religious enemies—as a unified front against "the Christian menace." Christians were hardly unique in being a persecuted Jewish sect. As one might expect, religious clashes between groups that, although holding to widely diverse philosophies, shared so many things in common was inevitable. We can compare these struggles to those between siblings who are close in age. It is clear from the available evidence that Judaism was marred by religious infighting that often led to violence and bloodshed. This was not limited to Pharisaical attacks on Christianity as with the Pharisee Paul's zealous assaults on the new sect (Acts 9:1–3; 1 Cor 15:9). For example, the Sadducean high priest, Alexander Janneus (in office 103–76 BC), had 800 Pharisees crucified and ordered their wives and children to be executed before their eyes as they died on their crosses (Josephus, *Ant* 13.380–83). In addition, Josephus narrates the brutal sectarian violence that took place between various Zealot groups during the Jerusalem siege (*JW* 5.248–57). Imagine, the Romans are outside the walls of Jerusalem and the Zealots are too busy killing each other to notice them!

In addition to "normal" sectarian differences, it is reasonable to think that the Christian impulse to convert others to their way of thinking itself led to difficulties. For example, Paul's evangelistic strategy, as described by Acts, lent itself to problems. According to Acts, when Paul came to a new town he would go to the local synagogue and attempt to convert the Jews to Christianity. His particular brand of Christianity seems to have been more popular with those Greek adherents to Judaism than with the Jews themselves.

His "stealing" of these Greek adherents did not make him popular with the Jews. Paul's theological differences with his fellow Jews often degenerated into loud and violent arguments, which sometimes ended in bloodshed (cf. Paul's own description of his sufferings in 2 Cor 11:24–7). Other examples of such clashes ending in bloodshed are provided by the account in Acts of the stoning of Stephen (6:8–7:60) and also the fourth century Church historian, Eusebius' account of the martyrdom of James, the head of the Church at Jerusalem (ca. AD 62; *Ecclesiastical History* 2.23). It is interesting to note here that while Eusebius presents testimony from the second century Church father, Hegesippus, that implicates the *scribes and Pharisees* as engineers of the death of James, he also includes the account of Josephus, who specifically and unequivocally implicates the new *Sadducean* High Priest, Ananus in James' death. In fact, Josephus notes, "those of the city [Jerusalem] that seemed the most moderate and most accurate in observing the law, were greatly offended by this" (2.23.23; cf. Josephus, *Ant* 20.197–203). If Josephus is correct, it may have been that the Pharisees of Jerusalem were actually outraged by the execution of James, perceived by them to be amenable to their way of thinking, and not at all complicit in his death. Hegesippus' ascription of James' death to the "scribes and Pharisees" may reflect historically later tensions such as those captured in the late first century Gospels of Matthew (e.g., chapter 23) and John (e.g., 9:13–23).

Perceived from the Roman point of view, these religious clashes between Jews and Christians eventually involved threats to the greater social order. To the Roman mind upheaval and social unrest led to rioting, this was tantamount to rebellion. Since the Romans were essentially an occupying power, they could not allow social unrest—even that predicated on religious and not specifically political dissention. Therefore, it would be in the Romans' best interest to intervene and crush the causes of the unrest before they could rise to crisis level. We see precisely this kind of thing happening in Acts 21:27—23:10.

In light of accounts like those of the martyrdom of Stephen and the subsequent persecution in Jerusalem described in Acts 8:1–3, one might easily imagine that persecution was widespread and that many were killed for the faith in the early period. However, the larger picture in the New Testament does not support this idea. Certainly, there are the stories of the executions of Stephen and James the brother of John (Acts 12:2), the oblique reference to Peter's violent death (John 21:18) and Paul's description of his own sufferings at the hands of both Jews and Gentiles (2 Cor 11:24–25). On the other hand, the Book of Revelation presents a very interesting picture of the situations faced by the seven churches in Asia Minor (modern western Turkey) it purports to address. As one reads through the letters to these seven churches found in chapters 2 and 3, a surprising realization emerges. In Ephesus the main focus is on the threat posed by the Christian sect called the Nicolaitans (2:6). In Smyrna, there is mention of Jewish pressure (2:9). John seems to suspect that there will be an impending imprisonment of some Christians, which he believes will end in their deaths (2:10–11). However, this has not happened yet at the time these letters were written and, for all we know, may never have occurred at all! In Pergamum, the church has suffered at least one martyrdom (Antipas), yet here again the main focus is on John's attack against despised groups of *other Christians*, associated respectively with Balaam (2:14) and the Nicolaitans (2:15). This hardly sounds like a church under siege! Likewise, the church in Thyatira is warned about a Christian woman prophetess and teacher, slanderously called "Jezebel" (2:20–25). Sardis is described as "sleeping" (3:1), hardly a proper metaphor to describe a church under attack. The letter to Philadelphia mentions Jewish pressure (3:8–10) yet makes no reference to executions or violence. Lastly, Laodicea is described as a Christian church that is prosperous and complacent with no whisper of a threat on the horizon. All in all, the evidence from Revelation does not reveal a situation where Christians are hunted. Rather, the single biggest threat seems to be from other Christian groups within the churches that hold differing views!

Thus it seems proper to say that during the initial spread of Christianity, persecution was a local (as opposed to empire-wide) phenomenon and that it appears to have affected only a few, more vocal Christian leaders. The latter of these two conditions would change in with the infamous Neronic Persecution. (However, it should be stressed here that even this was really just a local persecution as there is no specific evidence that this persecution reached beyond the city limits of Rome.)

FIGURE 24

The Neronic Persecution began as a political response to a fire that ravaged the city of Rome. On the evening of July 18, AD 64, a fire broke out in Rome that burned for six days and seven nights and resulted in the destruction of three entire quarters of Rome. Thousands were made homeless by the fire. The Emperor's response to this catastrophe was swift. As soon as he heard of the fire Nero, who was at Antium at the time, rushed back to Rome and began to organize relief efforts. Public buildings, the Field of Mars and his own Vatican Gardens were made available for the displaced victims of the raging inferno. In addition, Nero saw to it that food was brought from Ostia and several of the neighboring towns.

FIGURE 25

As in many times of national crisis, the population looked for someone to blame and naturally settled on their political leader, Nero (**see Figure 24**). Rumor had it that Nero was so moved by the sight of Rome burning that he donned his singer's robes and played the lyre, singing through a tragic song that he himself had composed, *The Fall of Troy*. This is the basis behind the saying that Nero "fiddled while Rome burned." Still other things suggested a high-level conspiracy as reports came in that roving gangs of thugs were hindering the firefighting efforts. While it is possible that Nero may have had the fire set so as to clear the way for a large-scale building project, this seems unlikely given the fact that the fire began very far away from the area Nero had targeted for renovation. As with most disasters, theories abound as to the involvement of government officials. The Roman historian Suetonius directly points to Nero as the author of this tragedy. On the other hand, the Roman historian Tacitus chooses to suspend judgment. In all fairness it must be stated that definite conclusions as to the true cause of the fire are hard to draw from the limited and biased information available.

What can be asserted as factual is that Nero realized from the public mood against him that he needed a scapegoat for the fire. He found a perfect group of victims in the Roman Christians. Tacitus describes the resultant persecution in *Annals* 15.44:

> Consequently, to get rid of the report, Nero fastened the guilt and inflicted the most exquisite tortures on a class hated for their abominations, called Christians by the populace. Christus, from whom the name had its origin, suffered the extreme penalty during the reign of Tiberius at the hands of one of our procurators, Pontius Pilatus, and a most mischievous superstition, thus checked for the moment, again broke out not only in Judea, the first source of the evil, but even in Rome, where all things hideous and shameful from every part of the world find their center and become popular. Accordingly, an arrest was first made of all who pleaded guilty; then, upon their information, an immense multitude was convicted, not so much of the crime of firing the city, as of hatred against mankind. Mockery of every sort was added to their deaths. Covered with the skins of beasts, they were torn by dogs and perished, or were nailed to crosses, or were doomed to the flames and burnt, to serve as a nightly illumination, when daylight had expired.
>
> Nero offered his gardens for the spectacle, and was exhibiting a show in the circus, while he mingled with the people in the dress of a charioteer or stood aloft on a car. Hence, even for criminals who deserved extreme and exemplary punishment, there arose a feeling of compassion; for it was not, as it seemed, for the public good, but to glut one man's cruelty, that they were being destroyed.

According to tradition, Peter and Paul were among those who lost their lives under Nero. The earliest available accounts (highly idealized) of these executions are found in the mid to late second century apocryphal *Acts of Peter* 30–41 and *Acts of Paul* 11.1–7. Later, Eusebius (*Hist. eccl.* 2.25) affirms the basic traditions of the two key apostles' deaths under Nero (i.e., Paul's beheading and Peter's crucifixion). There are a number of monuments in Rome that commemorate the events surrounding the violent deaths of these two apostles (**see Figures 25–27**). However, it should be noted here that neither the apocryphal acts nor Eusebius link the apostles' deaths

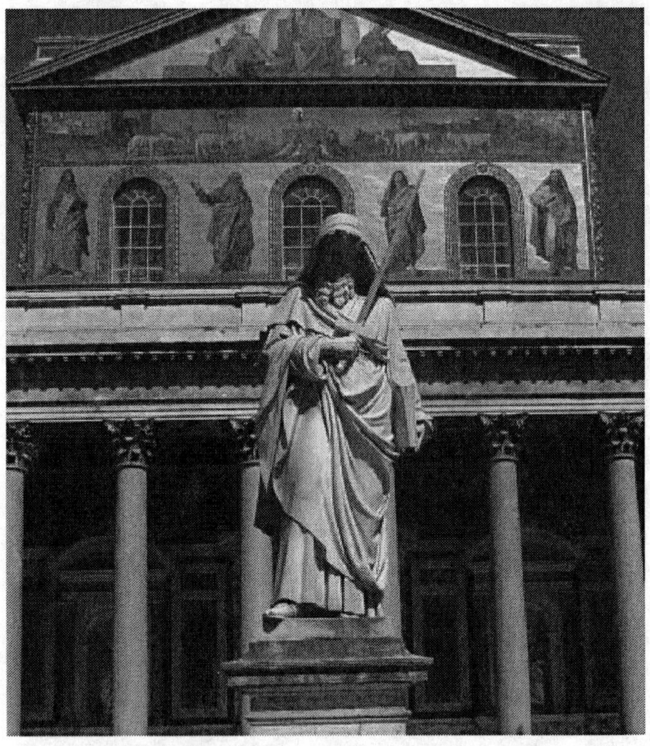

FIGURE 26

with the Great Fire of AD 64. While the accounts in the apocryphal acts can hardly be considered reliable history, it is interesting that in the *Acts of Peter*, Peter *alone* is executed, being targeted as one who was regarded as a "trouble-maker" (*Acts of Peter* 34). Further, the *Acts of Peter* presents a Roman prefect named Agrippa as the direct cause of Peter's death, not Nero (chapter 36). Therefore, it is not outside the realm of possibility that this apostle was killed at some earlier or later date and not as part of the general purge of AD 64. On the other hand, the *Acts of Paul* clearly sets Paul's beheading in the context of a general assault of Nero on the larger Christian community (chapter 11.2–3).

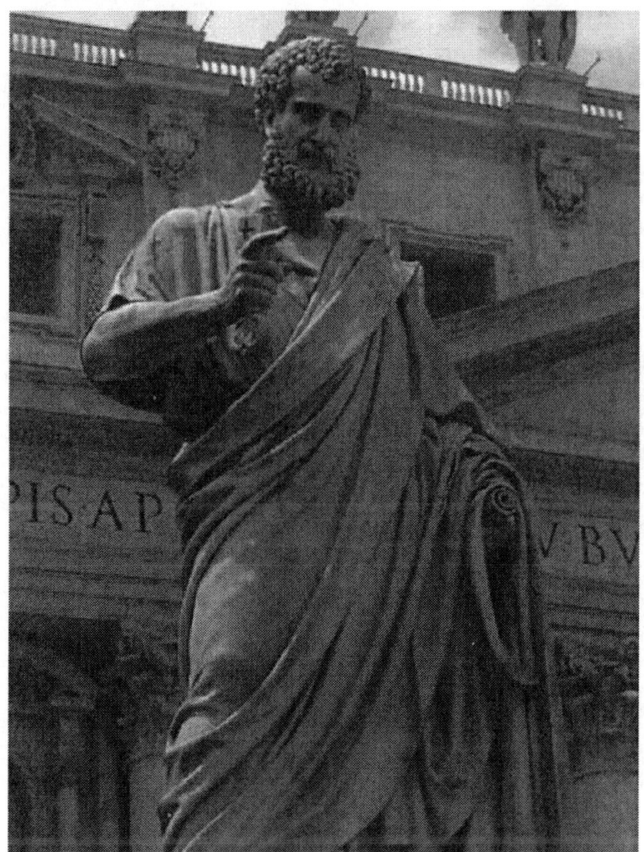

FIGURE 27

Moving beyond the actual persecution itself, we can observe that there appear to be clues within Tacitus' account of this persecution that reveal a prevailing anti-Christian sentiment. In particular, there are two phrases that attract particular attention in this regard. Christians are said to be "hated for their abominations" by the populace and thought to be guilty of "hatred of mankind." What do these statements mean and what can they tell us about the societal causes of this persecution? Are they just offhanded insults or do they have "content"?

Some light may be shed on the first phrase ("hated for their abominations") by reading the work of the North African Christian writer, Minucius Felix. In his work the *Octavius* (ca. 218–235), Minucius Felix presents a debate between his two friends, a fellow convert to Christianity, Octavius Januarius, and the non-Christian, Caecilius Natalis. The debate, which takes place on the seashore of the Roman port city, Ostia, is an attempt to record and then answer typical objections to Christianity. In the course of this dispute the non-Christian, Caecilius, launches into an attack on Christianity that captures a sense of some of the common opinions current in the early third century. While it must be admitted that this document represents opinions held approximately 150 years after the Neronic Persecution, it is likely, based on the nature of the accusations, that Caecilius' words accurately reflect the "abominations" assumed by the wider Roman public to be part and parcel of the Christian religion. The following are key segments drawn from Caecilius' attack on Christianity:

> 8.3 "In view of this, is it not an absolute scandal—you will allow me, I hope, to be rather forthright about the strong feelings I have for my case—is it not scandalous that the gods should be mobbed by a gang of outlawed and reckless desperadoes? 4. They have collected from the lowest possible dregs of society the more ignorant fools together with gullible women (readily persuaded, as is their weak sex); they have thus formed a rabble of blasphemous conspirators, who with nocturnal assemblies, periodic fasts, and inhuman feasts seal their pact not with some religious ritual but with desecrating profanation; they are a crowd that furtively lurks in hiding places, shunning the light; they are speechless in public but gabble away in corners.
>
> "They despise our temples as being no more than sepulchres, they spit after our gods, they sneer at our rites, and, fantastic though it is, our priests they pity—pitiable themselves; they scorn the purple robes of public office, though they go about in rags themselves. . . .

9.1. "Evil weeds grow apace and so, day by day, this depraved way of life now creeps further over all the face of the globe and the foul religious shrines of this abominable congregation are getting a stronger hold. This confederacy must be torn out, it must be sworn to perdition.

2. "They recognize each other by secret marks and signs; hardly have they met when they love each other, throughout the world uniting in the practice of a veritable religion of lusts. Indiscriminately they call each other brother and sister, thus turning even ordinary fornication into incest by the intervention of these hallowed names. Such a pride does this foolish, deranged superstition take in its wickedness.

3. "Unless there were some underlying truth, such a wide variety of charges, and very serious ones, would not be made about them; they can hardly be repeated in polite company. Rumor is a shrewd informant. I hear, for example, that they do reverence to the head of that most degraded of beasts, an ass; I cannot imagine what absurdity has persuaded them to consecrate it, but it is indeed a cult born of such morals and well suited for them. 4. It is also reported that they worship the genitals of their pontiff and priest, adoring, it appears, the sex of their 'father.' Perhaps this is incorrect but it certainly is a suspicion that befits their clandestine and nocturnal ceremonies. There are also stories about the objects of their veneration: they are said to be a man who was punished with death as a criminal and the fell wood of his cross, thus providing suitable liturgy for the depraved fiends: they worship what they deserve.

5. "To turn to another point. The notoriety of the stories told of the initiation of new recruits is matched by their ghastly horror. A young baby is covered over with flour, the object being to deceive the unwary. It is then served before the person to be admitted into their rites. The recruit is urged to inflict blows onto it—they appear to be harmless because of the covering of flour. Thus the baby is killed with wounds that remain unseen and concealed. It is the blood of this infant—I shudder to mention it—it is this blood that they lick with thirsty lips; these are the limbs they distribute eagerly; this is the victim by which they seal their covenant; it is by complicity in this crime that they are pledged to mutual silence; these are their rites, more foul than all sacrileges combined.

6. "We all know, too, about their banquets; they are on everyone's lips, everywhere as the speech of our Cirtensian testifies. On a special day they gather for a feast with all their children, sisters, mothers—all sexes and all ages. There, flushed with the banquet after such feasting and drinking, they begin to burn with incestuous passions. They provoke a dog tied to the lampstand to leap and bound towards a scrap of food which they have tossed outside the reach of his chain.

7. "By this means the light is overturned and extinguished, and with it common knowledge of their actions; in the shameless dark with unspeakable lust they copulate in random unions, all equally being guilty of incest, some by deed, but everyone by complicity. For whatever may happen in individual cases is the general aspiration and desire of them all." (8.3–4; 9.1–7)

From this appalling assault we can discern three major "abominations" that were used to smear the Christian reputation: atheism, sexual immorality (with a particular emphasis on incest) and cannibalism. We shall now examine each of these charges in detail so as to better grasp their relevance for the early Church.

Atheism

Roman religion was largely corporate and legalistic. By corporate, I mean that religion was viewed as a relationship that was forged between the state as an entity and the gods, i.e., the gods in relationship with Rome as opposed to in relationship with individuals. By legalistic, I mean that the Romans felt a need to fulfill obligations between themselves and the gods. It was simply a matter of determining what it was that

FIGURE 28

the gods required and then meticulously fulfilling those requests. For example, if Mars asked for three sacrifices per year, then Mars must receive three sacrifices per year. The gods must be appeased. In short, the purpose of Roman religion was to gain the good will of the gods and keep them benevolent toward Rome. The benevolence of the gods was thought to ensure the success and prosperity of the community and even the individual. In order to maintain this *pax deorum* or "peace with the gods" it was essential that the state and all its citizens establish and maintain a correct relationship with the gods (**see Figures 28–32**).

FIGURE 29

One could say that the driving forces behind Roman state religion can be summed up by two Latin words: *pietas* and *religio*. *Pietas* reflected a sense of fulfilling one's obligations and could be used in reference to the gods, the state, the family, etc. In the religious sphere *pietas* denoted a quality that resulted when one fulfilled ones obligations and duties toward the gods by performing rituals according to custom and the accepted rules of propriety. On the other hand, *religio* meant scruple or awe in the presence of the gods with an accompanying sense of uneasiness if one's obligations were not performed.

Despite its paranoia in regard to *pietas*, the Roman society was still fairly tolerant of foreign religions. Rome's position as capital city of a huge and demographically diverse empire and its high population of foreign-born slaves (perhaps one-fifth of the population) virtually ensured the presence of foreign religions. In the vast majority of cases, these religions were viewed with suspicion yet tolerated. These other religions did not interfere with the Roman state religion in that they allowed their worshippers to participate in more than one religion. However, there were several well-known historical examples of occasional Roman persecutions aimed

FIGURE 30

against foreign cults (e.g., the worshippers of Isis; Josephus, *Ant* 18.65–80 and the suppression of the Bacchanalia; Livy, *History of Rome* 4.254–59) including the Jews (during the reign of Tiberius; Suetonius, *The Twelve Caesars*: *Tiberius* 36; during the reign of Claudius, Suetonius *The Twelve Caesars*: *Claudius* 25). In these cases of persecution and suppression the motive was a perceived threat to the social order, whether that be political (e.g., possible sources of insurrection) or interpersonal (e.g., elite Roman women exercising unacceptable sexual license).

Now according to the character Caecilius in the *Octavius*, Christians are said to "despise our temples as being no more than sepulchres, they spit after our gods, they sneer at our rites." This charge, essentially that of *atheism*, is a very serious accusation in the mind of a traditional Roman. By disregarding and even deliberately offending the gods, the Christians could very well be bringing a world of hurt down on the Empire. Today we would call this compulsion to

FIGURE 31

fulfill religious rituals superstition but the Romans took such things very seriously. For example, in the first century BC the Roman poet Horace (65–8 BC) attributes the crushing military defeats (e.g., to the Parthians at Carrhae in 53 BC) and civil wars (i.e., Julius Caesar versus Pompey; Octavian and Antony versus the assassins of Caesar, Brutus and Cassius)

Rome had and was experiencing during that period to neglect of the state religion:

> You will continue to pay for your father's sins, O Roman, although you yourself are guiltless, until you have restored the temples and crumbling shrines of the gods and their statues, filthy with black smoke. You rule an empire because you acknowledge that you are subordinate to the gods. From them comes every beginning; attribute to them also every outcome. You have neglected the gods, and they have heaped on Italy many grievous calamities. (*Odes* 3.6.1–8; cf. also Livy, *History of Rome* 5.51)

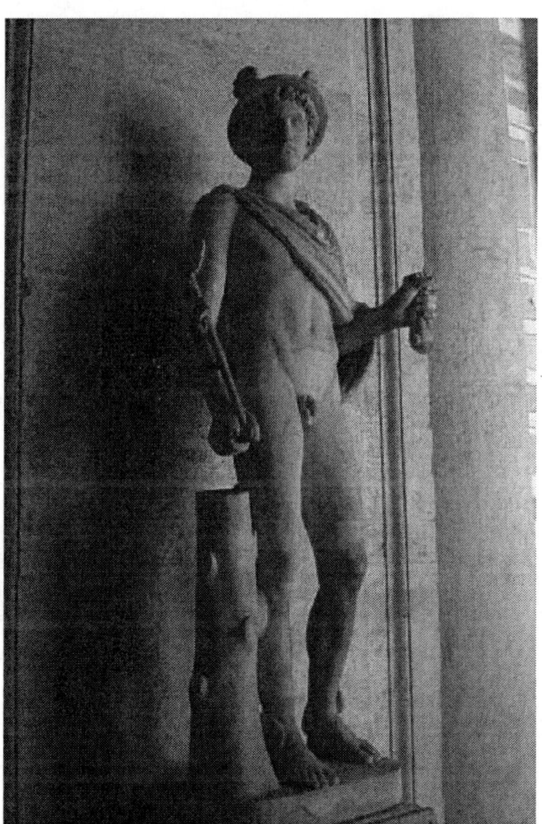

FIGURE 32

Similar statements by other ancient writers can be multiplied but Horace's point here is widely accepted: the proper appeasement of the gods is the cause of Roman political and military success. Once one understands this principle, it is not hard to understand why atheism would be such a serious charge. Not only could Christians' atheistic attitudes and behaviors threaten the Roman state but also the very refusal of Christians to participate in the state religion betrays an inherent lack of loyalty to the state. Taken together with the Christian terminology discussed above (i.e., "kingdom of God"; "Lord" and "soldiers of Christ"), suspicions were confirmed that the Christians were anti-Roman.

Sexual Immorality (Incest)

For anyone who knows much about Roman society, this is a particularly amusing charge—quite literally, the "pot calling the kettle black." In general, it should be understood that Greco-Roman society was permeated by an open and frank sexuality that would be considered crass even by modern American standards. As Roman society was a male dominated culture, this fixation on sex became yet another way for the Roman male to assert his power and authority. The sexual options open to elite Roman males included their wives (in order to produce legitimate children), courtesans (for romance), slaves of both sexes (to satisfy baser lusts) and even young boys. Most lower class Roman men commonly visited prostitutes, whose brothels, staffed by slaves of both sexes, were open to the public and were readily affordable.

In addition, it was commonplace within Roman culture to see the male sexual organ or *phallus,* which was believed to bring good luck and protection, prominently displayed. For example, women and children wore jewelry that unashamedly displayed the male reproductive organ and carried *phalli* of all shapes and sizes in religious processions. Elsewhere, the *phallus* could be found readily on plaques placed on the lintels of doorframes and walls and in the form of *herms*, vertical stone pillars topped with the head of the god Hermes and featuring his erect phallus on the shaft below. Depictions of even the most extreme sexual acts were used to adorn mirrors, drinking bowls, plates, oil lamps and many other ordinary household items. Sexuality even touched horticulture in Roman circles as it was common for a family garden to be guarded by a statue of the well-endowed Priapus, god of fertility and agriculture, whose inscriptions promised the direst of sexual fates for anyone who dared to rob from the garden in question.

Roman literature of all kinds was infused with sexual themes and those of the crudest type. The examples that can be named span the range of literature running from popular epigrams (e.g., the *Epigrams* of the first century AD poet, Martial), to novels (e.g., the *Satyricon*, written by the friend of Nero himself, Petronius Arbiter), to "how to" books (e.g., *The Art of Love*, a manual on how to commit adultery written by the poet, Ovid, 43 BC–AD 17) and poetry (e.g., the highly charged poems of the first century BC love poets, Catullus and Tibullus).

Much more could be said on this topic but suffice it here to say that Roman society was highly sexed. By saying this, I do not mean to claim that Christians were at all times and in every way innocent of such charges of sexual impropriety. Just as today, the early Church witnessed occasional sexual excess within its ranks. Paul himself, in 1 Corinthians, is forced to castigate his spiritual children for an incestuous relationship between a man and his father's wife (incestuous by "legal" standards and not biology; 5:1) and visiting prostitutes (6:15–20). Paul clearly states, "Do not be deceived! Fornicators, idolaters, adulterers, male prostitutes, sodomites, thieves, the greedy, drunkards, revilers, robbers—none of these will inherit the kingdom of God. And this is what some of you used to be" (1 Cor 6:9b–11a). We must agree that not only had the Corinthian Christians once engaged in sexual sin but also some were clearly continuing these past bad habits.

Putting aside what we can only hope were rare indiscretions, the Christian faith as a whole tended more toward sexual asceticism than sexual license. Jesus' own teaching as reported in the Gospels lays down strict standards of sexual conduct (e.g., Matt 5:27–30) and this teaching was echoed and reinforced by teachers like Paul (e.g., 1 Cor 7:1–7). In addition, popular Christian literature such as the second and third century apocryphal acts of the apostles strongly promote sexual continence.

Even if we examine the exact nature of the charges leveled by Caecilius in the *Octavius* we can see that the charge of incest is unfounded based on the evidence he provides (i.e., calling someone "brother" or "sister" is hardly enough evidence to convict someone). As for the description of the Christian "sex orgy," we can say that it probably has more in common with popular Roman practice than with Christian ritual. In general, we can regard these charges as inflated rumors concocted to defame the early Christians with little if any basis in fact.

Cannibalism

Without doubt this charge must stem from misconceptions and rumors related to the Christian practice of the Eucharist and Jesus' famous interpretation of the bread eaten in this memorial meal as his "body" and the wine imbibed as his "blood" (Mark 14:22–24). As this came to be elaborated upon by Christianity in texts like John 6 it became even more stark and shocking.

> I am the living bread that came down from heaven. Whoever eats of this bread will live forever; and the bread that I will give for the life of the world is my flesh." The Jews then disputed among themselves, saying, "How can this man give us his flesh to eat?" So Jesus said to them, "Very truly, I tell you, unless you eat the flesh of the Son of Man and drink his blood, you have no life in you. Those who eat my flesh and drink my blood have eternal life, and I will raise them up on the last day; for my flesh is true food and my blood is true drink. Those who eat my flesh and drink my blood abide in me, and I in them. (6:51–56; NRSV)

Even the Gospel of John itself notes that these words attributed to Jesus were found to be offensive among those who were his followers (6:59–66), causing a break within the community.

As far as early Christian relations with the larger Greco-Roman society were concerned, this accusation was probably the most damaging. Obviously, the average person living in a "civilized society" is not going to look too sympathetically on someone who is a cannibal. In addition, this charge is probably the most difficult to defend against. The reason for this is that for a Christian to answer a non-Christian's allegation honestly, the Christian must admit to eating the "Body of Christ." On hearing this "admission of guilt" there would be few people who would listen further as this Christian ritual was defended.

Now that we have fleshed out what Tacitus may have meant when he described Christianity as "a class hated for their abominations" we can proceed to interpreting his statement that Christians were guilty of "hatred against mankind."

Hatred against Mankind

Hatred against mankind or "*odium generis humani*" was a charge that was often applied by classical authors to the Jews. It involved not so much the desire to do personal damage but to turn one's back on obligations to one's fellows, and it was regarded as a characteristic fault of the Jewish community. In order to better understand this charge as it applied to the Jews of the Imperial period and, subsequently, to the Christians, we should recall that traditional Jewish religious practices would have necessitated a certain separation from the rest of society. For example, Jewish insistence on strict monotheism would have precluded any participation in the Roman civic cults. (The Romans granted the Jews exemptions from participation in the civic cult. This may well date from the mid-first century BC when, as a reward for Jewish support against the supporters of Ptolemy XII in 48 BC, Julius Caesar awarded special favors to the Jews.) This determination to maintain strict monotheistic standards would have hindered participation in various political functions as well as certain social events commonly held at Greek and Roman temples. In addition, Jewish dietary (kosher) considerations would have virtually eliminated any chance of Jews and Gentiles eating together, severely limiting social interaction between the two groups. Further, because of the desire to maintain cultural and religious integrity, Jews would have married only within their ethnic community, thereby preventing the formation of cross-cultural ties by marriage. These religious concerns would have had the effect of making the Jewish community appear standoffish, thus the perception that they "hated humanity."

Christians would have shared some of these same concerns. Christian refusal to acknowledge the significance or participate in the veneration of other gods would have had broad social ramifications. For example, Greco-Roman temples served as meeting places for ancient trade guilds (similar to modern unions). Christian refusal to enter these temples would preclude involvement in the guilds with all the attendant negative economic impact. These same temples also played a social role. Many temples had banqueting halls that were used by the ancients for some of the same purposes that modern church halls now serve. Refusal to enter these temples would thus also have a negative impact on familial relations. In addition, the fact that the athletic games, chariot races and gladiatorial games were dedicated to the gods would also raise significant concerns in the minds of the early Christians about the appropriateness of attending such events. (Hopefully, in the case of the gladiatorial events the more pressing concern would be the acts of murder that occurred within the arena.) Religious concerns would have also had ramifications in regard to Christian involvement in local and Imperial politics. Because of the necessity of participating in the Roman civic cult (as well as the potential inherent job requirement that a magistrate might have to impose the death penalty), socially elite Christians were discouraged from holding public office, a stance that would have made them appear hostile and unconcerned toward society as a whole.

Christian emphasis on morality (especially involving sexuality) would have had to play a role in further isolating the young religion. The theater often played host to live sex shows and many ancient plays both tragic and comedic were highly charged with sexual themes. For example, the famous play, *Oedipus Rex*, written by the great Greek playwright, Sophocles, is the story of an infant boy, abandoned and exposed by his parents, who grows up to murder, albeit unwittingly, his father and marry his mother. Similarly, much of Roman comedy is not unlike an ancient version of the 1970's television comedy, *Three's Company*, laced with sexual humor and innuendo.

These religious and ethical reservations would have had the effect of making Christians appear to be hostile to society at large. This reality is reflected in the words of the non-Christian, Caecilius, in Minucius Felix's *Octavius*:

> . . . in your anxious state of expectation, you refrain from honest pleasures: you do not go to our shows, you take no part in our processions, you are not present at our public banquets, you shrink in horror from our sacred games, from food ritually dedicated by our priests, from drink hallowed by libation poured upon our altars. Such is your dread of the very gods you deny. You do not bind your head with flowers, you do not honor, your body with perfumes; ointments you reserve for funerals, but even to your tombs you deny garlands; you anemic, neurotic creatures, you indeed deserve to be pitied-but by our gods. The result is, you pitiable fools, that you have no enjoyment of life while you wait for the new life, which you will never have . . . (12.5–6).

Part 3
The Roman Authorities and Their Response

With these thoughts our consideration of the "abominations" committed by the early Christians is concluded. Yet a major question remains: If the statements found in the *Octavius* are generally representative of the kinds of slanderous accusations that were leveled against the early Church by the general populace, what weight did these things have in the minds of the Roman governmental officials who were charged with the task of dealing with the Christians brought before their tribunals?

Figure 33

In order to begin to address this question, it is helpful to examine the correspondence between one Pliny the Younger and the Emperor Trajan (**see Figure 33**). Pliny (ca. AD 62–113) was appointed to the post of governor of Bithynia (located on the Black Sea coast of modern Turkey) in AD 111 or 112 and a collection of his Epistles remains to this day. In addition to providing a window into the daily activities of a provincial governor, Pliny's letters also provide a first person account of the tragic catastrophe of August 24, AD 79, when Mount Vesuvius (near modern Naples, Italy) erupted, burying the towns of Pompeii and Herculaeum under a blanket of volcanic ash. More importantly for our purposes, Pliny's letters also contain the first available discussion about the "Christian problem" between Roman officials—a governor and the emperor no less! The following includes both Pliny's letter to Trajan and the Emperor's response:

Letter 97; Pliny to the Emperor Trajan

It is my custom to refer all my difficulties to you, Sir, for no one is better able to resolve my doubts and inform my ignorance.

I have never been present at an examination of Christians. Consequently, I do not know the nature or the extent of the punishments usually meted out to them, nor the grounds for starting an investigation and how far it should be pressed. Nor am I at all sure whether any distinction should be made between them on grounds of age, or if young people and adults should be treated alike; whether a pardon ought to be granted to anyone retracting his beliefs, or if once he has professed Christianity, he shall gain nothing by renouncing it; and whether it is the mere name of Christian which is punishable, even if innocent of crime, or rather the crimes associated with the name.

For the moment this is the line I have taken with all persons brought before me on the charge of being Christians. I have asked them in person if they are Christians, and if they admit it, I repeat the question a second and a third time, with a warning of the punishment awaiting them. If they persist, I order them to be led away for execution; for, whatever the nature of their admission, I am convinced that their stubbornness and unshakeable obstinacy ought not to go unpunished. There have been others similarly fanatical who are Roman citizens. I have entered them on the list of persons to be sent to Rome for trial.

Now that I have begun to deal with this problem, as so often happens, the charges are becoming more widespread and increasing in variety. An anonymous pamphlet has been circulated which contains the names of a number of accused persons. Among these I considered that I should dismiss any who denied that they were or ever had been Christians when they repeated after me a formula of invocation to the gods and made offerings of wine and incense to your statue (which I had ordered to be brought into court for this purpose along with the images of the gods), and furthermore had reviled the name of Christ: none of which things, I understand, any genuine Christian can be induced to do.

Others, whose names were given to me by an informer, first admitted the charge and then denied it; they said they had ceased to be Christians two or more years previously, and some of them even twenty years ago. They all did reverence to your statue and the images of the gods in the same way as the others, and reviled the name of Christ. They also declared that the sum total of their guilt or error amounted to no more than this: they had met regularly before dawn on a fixed day to chant verses alternately among themselves in honor of Christ as if to a god, and also to bind themselves by oath, not for any criminal purpose, but to abstain from theft, robbery and adultery, to commit no breach of trust and not to deny a deposit when called upon to restore it. After this ceremony it had been their custom to disperse and reassemble later to take food of an ordinary, harmless kind; but they had in fact given up this practice since my edict, issued on your instructions, which banned all political societies. This made me decide it was all the more necessary to extract the truth by torture from two slave-women, whom they call deaconesses. I found nothing but a degenerate sort of cult carried to extravagant lengths.

I have therefore postponed any further examination and hastened to consult you.

> The question seems to me to be worthy of your consideration, especially in view of the number of persons endangered; for a great many individuals of every age and class, both men and women, are being brought to trial, and this is likely to continue. It is not only in towns, but villages and rural districts too which are infected through contact with this wretched cult. I think though that it is still possible for it to be checked and directed to better ends, for there is no doubt that people have begun to throng the temples which had been almost entirely deserted for a long time; the sacred rites which had been allowed to lapse are being performed again, and flesh of sacrificial victims is on sale everywhere, though up till recently scarcely anyone could be found to buy it. It is easy to infer from this that a great many people could be reformed if they were given an opportunity to repent.

LETTER 98; THE EMPEROR TRAJAN TO PLINY

> You have followed the right course of procedure, my dear Pliny, in your examination of the cases of persons charged with being Christians, for it is impossible to lay down a general rule to a fixed formula. These people must not be hunted out; if they are brought before you and the charge against them is proved, they must be punished, but in the case of anyone who denies that he is a Christian, and makes it clear that he is not by offering prayers to our gods, he is to be pardoned as a result of his repentance however suspect his past conduct may be. But pamphlets circulated anonymously must play no part in any accusation. They create the worst sort of precedent and are quite out of keeping with the spirit of our age.

This letter of Pliny is rather depressing from a Christian point of view in that it mentions a number of Christians who have apostatized from the faith (i.e., denied their faith when faced with persecution). Pliny states: "Others, whose names were given to me by an informer, first admitted the charge and then denied it; they said they had ceased to be Christians two or more years previously, and some of them even twenty years ago. They all did reverence to your statue and the images of the gods in the same way as the others, and reviled the name of Christ." Sadly, apostasies were a common problem as the early Christians faced the tortures and brutal executions of the Romans. Not only does Pliny's letter to Trajan (our earliest non-Christian Imperial witness) mention Christians who denied their faith but this reality is also attested by some of the earliest and most respected accounts of the martyrs.

FIGURE 34

The *Martyrdom of Polycarp*, the account of the execution of the aged bishop of Smyrna (modern Turkey) ca. 155–60, tells in chapter 4 of a man named Quintus who "when he saw the wild animals he turned cowardly." The *Martyrdom* explains how the governor "used many arguments and persuaded him to swear by the gods and offer sacrifice." In addition, the *Letter of the Churches of Lyons and Vienne*, written by the communities of Lyons and Vienne in Gaul (France) to the churches of Asia and Phrygia (modern Turkey), relates similar occurrences. This letter (dated ca. 177), which is now found in the work of the church historian Eusebius, *Hist. eccl.* 5.1.3–2.8, recounts how some Christians "were shown to be still untrained, unprepared, and weak, unable to bear the strain of a great conflict. Of these about ten in all were stillborn, causing us great grief and measureless distress . . ." (5.1.11). Still, worse was yet to come.

The Persecution of Decius (ca. 249–51; **see Figure 34**) was infamous for its apostasies! In late 249, the one-time legionary commander Decius, who had only recently attained the position of emperor through military force, sought to bring about a heightened sense of unity within the Empire by requiring everyone to offer sacrifice to the traditional gods. The results were absolutely devastating to the Christian communities. Despite the courageous martyrdoms of important Church leaders such as Bishop Fabian of Rome, Bishop Alexander of Jerusalem and Bishop Babylas of Antioch (*Hist. eccl.* 6.39.2–5), many Christians readily performed the sacrifice or obtained a certificate stating they had done so by means of bribery or in some other illegal fashion. The treatises and epistles of the great Bishop Cyprian of Carthage, who was forced to flee to the desert outside of Carthage in order to direct his beleaguered church, tell of how even the Church's hierarchy was guilty of apostasy (see *On the Lapsed* 6 and *Epistles* 59.10; 65.3 and 67).

Beside evidence of widespread apostasy, another point can be gleaned from Pliny's letter to Trajan. Pliny's interviews of those Christians who had apostatized uncover no actual evidence of wrongdoing. The explanation of Christian ritual he received seemed so innocent that he suspected the sources ("This made me decide it was all the more necessary to extract the truth by torture from two slave-women . . ."). He resorts to the "old" ways of torture to attain accurate information. It is clear from his letter that Pliny cannot find evidence of actual crimes and so must justify his executions by blaming the victims' "stubbornness and unshakeable obstinacy" which to Pliny's mind "ought not to go unpunished."

Obviously, the Emperor does not think that the Christians are guilty of any real crimes either. He tells Pliny, "These people must not be hunted out." I suspect that this is because of the great bureaucratic strain that any persecution would put on the Roman Imperial resources. In order to pursue effectively those known or suspected Christians, soldiers must be diverted from their normal tasks of defense, patrol, and road construction to hunt down a "phantom threat."

It is blatantly obvious to me that the Roman authorities do *not* take the typical criminal accusations of cannibalism, atheism, etc. seriously. If they did, they would not allow for a policy that is outlined by Trajan —"Repentance equals acquittal." This is *never* the case in Roman criminal courts. Imagine how ridiculous it would be if a murderer was pardoned just for denying his status as a murderer! This very critique of Trajan's policy is set forth brilliantly by the Church Father Tertullian of Carthage (ca. 160–225) in *1 Apology* 2.

> And then, too, you do not in that case deal with us in the ordinary way of judicial proceedings against offenders; for, in the case of others denying, you apply the torture to make them confess—Christians alone you torture, to make them deny; whereas, if we were guilty of any crime, we should be sure to deny it, and you with your tortures would force us to confession. Nor indeed should you hold that our crimes require no such investigation merely on the ground that you are convinced by our confession of the name that the deeds were done,—*you* who are daily wont, though you know well enough what murder is, none the less to extract from the confessed murderer a full account of how the crime was perpetrated. So that with all the greater perversity you act, when, holding our crimes proved by our confession of the name of Christ, you drive us by torture to fall from our confession, that, repudiating the name, we may in like manner repudiate also the crimes with which, from that same

> confession, you had assumed that we were chargeable. I suppose, though you believe us to be the worst of mankind, you do not wish us to perish. For thus, no doubt, you are in the habit of bidding the murderer deny, and of ordering the man guilty of sacrilege to the rack if he persevere in his acknowledgment! Is that the way of it? . . . Well, you think the Christian a man of every crime, an enemy of the gods, of the emperor, of the laws, of good morals, of all nature; yet you compel him to deny, that you may acquit him, which without his denial you could not do. You play fast and loose with the laws. You wish him to deny his guilt that you may, even against his will, bring him out blameless and free from all guilt in reference to the past! Whence is this strange perversity on your part? How is it you do not reflect that a spontaneous confession is greatly more worthy of credit than a compelled denial; or consider whether, when compelled to deny, a man's denial may not be in good faith, and whether acquitted, he may not, then and there, as soon as the trial is over, laugh at your hostility, a Christian as much as ever?

I am convinced that the heart of the matter has to do with Roman insistence that all people submit to the ultimate authority of Rome. This relates back to Pliny's reference to the Christians' "contumacious and inflexible obstinacy." Such a direct challenge to the absolute authority of Rome could not be allowed. It was simply too dangerous a precedent.

Part 4 Punishments of Roma: Suffering for the Sake of the "Name"

As is demonstrated by Tacitus' account of the Neronic Persecution and Pliny's letter to Trajan, Christians were subject to both tortures in order to extract information and, upon confession of Christ, execution. It is my intention here to outline briefly several of the primary ways in which the Romans punished the Christians. I do this not to glorify the inhuman violence inflicted but rather so as not to dishonor the martyrs by glossing over their sufferings for the sake of "the Name." Along with each punishment, I will indicate where key examples can be found in the primary sources.

Carcer: The "Dark Hole"

The Latin word for "prison" is *carcer*, which means "an enclosure or enclosed place." Roman prisons were not used to punish criminals as time in prison is used to punish criminals today. Instead prisons served only to hold people awaiting trial or execution. Those who disobeyed court magistrates could also be imprisoned. The wealthy were generally held under house arrest at the home of a friend who would guarantee their presence at the trial. An example of the use of house

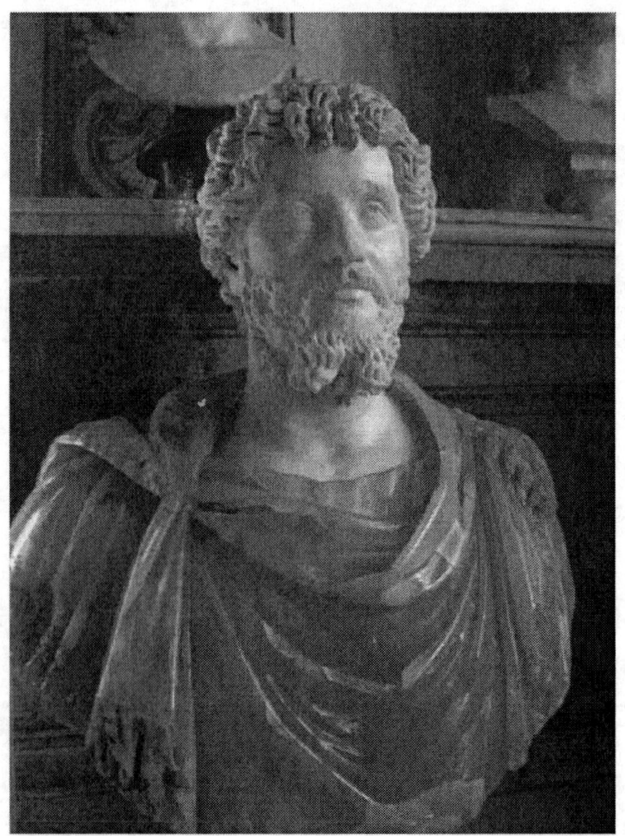

Figure 35

arrest with a wealthy Christian is that of Perpetua, a young Christian woman who was executed along with several other Christian companions on March 7, 203, in Carthage, North Africa during the reign of Septimius Severus (see *Martyrdom of Perpetua and Felicitas* 3; **see Figure 35**).

Roman prisons bore little resemblance to their modern counterparts. Prisons were often little more than subterranean storage facilities with little or no light and ventilation. In the aforementioned *Martyrdom of Perpetua and Felicitas* 3, Perpetua herself describes how she and her companions were moved to the prison and her shock at its terrible conditions:

> A few days later we were lodged in the prison; and I was terrified, as I had never before been in such a dark hole. What a difficult time it was! With the crowd the heat was stifling . . .

Perpetua's description of the prison conditions is echoed by Tertullian in his famous work, *To the Martyrs*, which some scholars believe was actually addressed to Perpetua and her companions. In Tertullian's attempt to encourage his fellow Christians, he mentions each of the difficulties of the prison in turn and then attempts to show how the Christian overcomes each of these obstacles:

> Other things, hindrances equally of the soul, may have accompanied you as far as the prison gate, to which also your relatives may have attended you. There and thenceforth you were severed from the world; how much more from the ordinary course of worldly life and all its affairs! Nor let this separation from the world alarm you; for if we reflect that the world is more really the prison, we shall see that you have gone out of a prison rather than into one. The world has the greater darkness, blinding men's hearts. The world imposes the more grievous fetters, binding men's very souls. The world breathes out the worst impurities—human lusts. The world contains the larger number of criminals, even the whole human race. Then, last of all, it awaits the judgment, not of the proconsul, but of God. Wherefore, O blessed, you may regard yourselves as having been translated from a prison to, we may say, a place of safety. It is full of darkness, but you yourselves are light; it has bonds, but God has made you free. Unpleasant exhalations are there, but you are an odor of sweetness. The judge is daily looked for, but you shall judge the judges themselves. Sadness may be there for him who sighs for the world's enjoyments. The Christian outside the prison has renounced the world, but in the prison he has renounced a prison too. It is of no consequence where you are in the world —you who are not of it. And if you have lost some of life's sweets, it is the way of business to suffer present loss that after gains may be the larger.

FIGURE 36

Some Christians died while in any one of the notorious Roman prisons (known for their horrible conditions), either awaiting trial or execution (e.g., a companion of Perpetua named Secundulus and another Christian taken during the same persecution named Quintus; see *Martyrdom of Perpetua and Felicitas* 14 and 11 respectively). In certain instances it appears that martyrs were condemned to starve to death while in prison (see Cyprian, *Ep.* 22). While in prison, the martyrs were dependent on the charity of their fellow Christians (e.g., Tertullian, *To the Martyrs* 1). In this regard, a key concern was the ability of the Christians to bribe the prison guards so as to gain access to their fellow believers.

The Carcer Tullianum or Mammertine Prison, the most famous Roman prison, can still be visited today. It is located just outside the Roman Forum, on the eastern slope of the Capitoline Hill. Historians believe that it was Ancus Marcius, the fourth king of Rome, who, sometime during his reign (640–616 BC) had constructed this dark, damp and foreboding subterranean structure. Originally, when a prisoner entered the prison, access was gained by first coming to a small room with a hole in the floor (**see Figure 36**). This hole was the sole entrance into the prison cell itself. Prisoners were thrown through this hole into the cell below, a room, 6 1/2 feet high, thirty feet long, and twenty-two feet wide. Today, this portal is covered with an iron grate. Visitors can access the cell proper by climbing down a flight of stone steps. Ancient Christian tradition says that both Peter and Paul were among the famous people who spent their last days there.

Banishment and Confiscation of Property

In Roman antiquity the regulations associated with imprisonment were lax. Sometimes magistrates delayed arrest to allow time for a person accused of a serious crime to go into voluntary exile (*exsilium*) before sentence could be pronounced. This allowed the accused to escape execution at the cost of both their citizenship and their property. In addition there were different types of banishment. For example, *relagatio* was temporary banishment to a location or exclusion from living in certain places and *deportatio* was perpetual banishment with the loss of citizenship and confiscation of all property. Exile was a punishment used largely for the upper classes. As such, banishment and the often-attendant confiscation of lands and goods were punishments of the Roman authorities that would be specifically injurious to those wealthy Christians who might consider confessing their faith.

The first time that banishment as a punishment for Christian belief and preaching is mentioned in Christian literature is found in the Book of Revelation 1:9, with John's claim to have been imprisoned for the sake of Christ Jesus:

> I, John, your brother who share with you in Jesus the persecution and the kingdom and the patient endurance, was on the island called Patmos because of the word of God and the testimony of Jesus.

Patmos is one of the Sporades Islands located in the Aegean Sea off the southwestern coast of Turkey. According to Pliny the Elder (*Natural History* 4.69–70) and Tacitus (*Annals* 4.30), three islands in the Sporades chain were used for exiles.

An interesting discussion of the very real possibility of Christians (in this case Roman Christians) having to face banishment and confiscation of goods is provided by the second-century Roman text, *Shepherd of Hermas, Par.* 1.1.1–6. The parable provides a metaphor of dual citizenship (the world and heaven) which lays out the negative ramifications of undue attachment to worldly riches and the peril of apostasy:

> He said to me: "You know," he said, "that you who are servants of God are living in a foreign country, for your city is far from this city. If, therefore, you know," he said, "your city in which you are destined to live, why do you prepare fields and expensive possessions and buildings and useless rooms here? The one who prepares these things for this city, therefore, does not plan to return to his own city. Foolish and double-minded and miserable man, don't you realize that all these things are foreign to you, and under someone else's authority? For the lord of this city will say, "I don't want you to live in my city; instead, leave this city, because you do not conform to my laws." So, you who have fields and dwellings and many other possessions, what will

> you do with your field and your house and all the other things you have prepared for yourself when you are expelled by him? For the lord of this country has every right to say to you, "Either conform to my laws, or get out of my country." So what are you going to do, since you are subject to the law of your own city? For the sake of your fields and the rest of your possessions, will you totally renounce your own law and live according to the law of this city? Take care; it may not be in your best interest to renounce your own law, for if you should want to return to your city, you will certainly not be accepted, because you have renounced the law of your city, and will be shut out of it."

On a somewhat related note, the Roman historian, Dio Cassius (*Roman History* 67.14) describes a period of persecution in Rome under the Emperor Domitian (emperor from AD 81–96). While this persecution probably predated the *Shepherd of Hermas* by several decades, this passage, traditionally suspected to refer to persecution of Christians, is significant because it also mentions the confiscation of property.

> And the same year Domitian slew, along with many others, Flavius Clemens the consul, although he was a cousin and had to wife Flavia Domitilla, who was also a relative of the emperor's. The charge brought against them both was that of atheism, a charge on which many others who drifted into Jewish ways were condemned. Some of these were put to death, and the rest were at least deprived of their property.

The *Epistles* of Cyprian, bishop of Carthage, North Africa, discuss the reality of this punishment as faced by Carthaginian Christians during the middle of the third century (see *Ep.* 24 and 25).

The Arena: Sands of Death

Of course, not all Christians were wealthy or part of the elite Roman families. For many Christian martyrs the various Roman arenas became the places in which they gasped out their last breaths (**see Figures 37–44**). The Roman arena as an institution has some connections with modern sports stadiums. Its affairs were called *munera* or games and were promoted by advertisements in public places which provided details of upcoming events. Even smaller points of similarity intersect. For example, it was not uncommon in the arena for slaves to come out during periods of lull between events and throw out wooden balls called *missilia*, each marked with a different number. These balls were redeemable for various prizes ranging in worth from modest gifts of food, grain or animals to larger prizes such as money, slaves and properties. Anyone who has ever attended a major or minor league baseball game or even an arena football contest knows that this practice is still going strong.

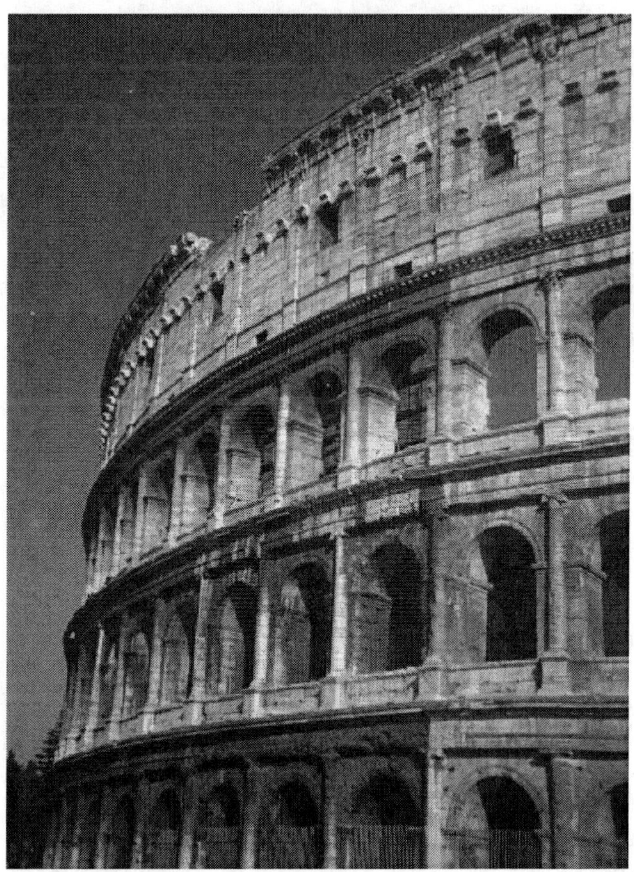

Figure 37

Despite the many points of similarity the arena was also unlike our games in that people came to see other human beings and animals die public and brutal deaths. A day at the arena would generally unfold something like this:

After the various opening ceremonies (which I shall not elucidate here) and when the crowd was all seated, the day's games began. Usually, the opening acts had a certain freakish or bizarre quality to them. Unlike the events to follow, these games had a relatively harmless character. Some of these acts were introductory fights which involved mock-fighters called *paegniarii* who fought with sticks and whips. Other mock combats involved fighters who fought with wooden weapons and were called the *lusorii*. The ranks of the *paegniarii* and the *lusorii* included cripples, dwarves, and even women. The Romans loved to laugh as dwarves squared off and battled each other.

FIGURE 38

Sometimes women were matched against each other in non-lethal exhibition or against dwarves—all of this done with a certain absurd sense of humor.

The second phase of the day's events was the *venationes* or wild beast hunts. The primary reference of this word was to actual hunts of game, some of dangerous predators, some of tamer species. In actual practice, the word *venationes* was an umbrella term that included other associated spectacles, such as displays of exotic species from conquered provinces, exhibitions of trained animals, fights between animals of different species or between animals and humans. Few people realize that the modern bullfights that take place in Mexico and her colonizing power Spain are the direct descendants of the Roman *venationes*.

Despite the cruelty and bloody nature of the *venationes*, there was one aspect of these spectacles that had a lighter side. Occasionally there would be shows of trained animals as in a modern circus. Seneca mentions such performances "... a trainer inserts his hand into the jaws of a lion, a keeper kisses his tiger, a very small Ethiopian orders an elephant to kneel down and to walk a tightrope" (*Ep*. 85.41). Sources also tell of other acts that were sometimes displayed such as dancing bears or of a lion trained to catch rabbits with its teeth and return them alive to its child master.

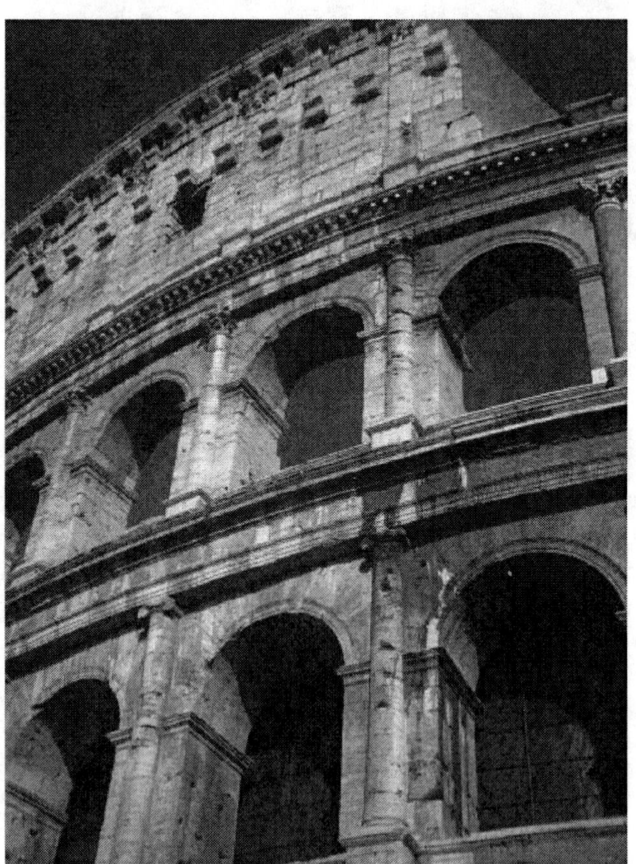

FIGURE 39

When the *venationes* concluded around midday, the public executions of the criminals or *noxii* began. It was at this point during the day that the Christians were executed. Despite the image suggested to us by Hollywood of Christians being executed before capacity crowds, it is probably more accurate to say that many in the audience would leave their seats and take this opportunity either to relieve themselves or to get something to eat from one of the many food vendors that plied their wares in the lower concourses of the arena. One could compare the draw of the midday executions to the mildly entertaining events that are scheduled during the intermissions between the periods of a minor league hockey game. As anyone

FIGURE 40

knows who has attended one of these contests, it is likely that better than half of the crowd has left their seats before these interim events even begin. The first century AD Roman philosopher Seneca describes these midday executions and his concerns for their impact on the observer (*Epistle* 7, *On the Crowds*)

> But nothing is so damaging to good character as the habit of lounging at the games; for then it is that vice steals subtly upon one through the avenue of pleasure. What do you think I mean? I mean that I come home more greedy, more ambitious, more voluptuous, and even more cruel and inhuman,—because I have been among human beings. By chance I attended a mid-day exhibition, expecting some fun, wit, and relaxation,—an exhibition at which men's eyes have respite from the slaughter of their fellow-men. But it was quite the reverse. The previous combats were the essence of compassion; but now all the trifling is put aside and it is pure murder. The men have no defensive armor. They are exposed to blows at all points, and no one ever strikes in vain. Many persons prefer this program to the usual pairs and to the bouts "by request." Of course they do; there is no helmet or shield to deflect the weapon. What is the need of defensive armor or skill? All these mean delaying death. In the morning they throw men to the lions and the bears; at noon, they throw them to the spectators. The spectators demand that the slayer shall face the man who is to slay him in his turn; and they always reserve the latest conqueror for another butchering. The outcome of every fight is death, and the means are fire and the sword. This sort of thing goes on while the arena is empty. You may retort: "But he was a highway robber; he killed a man!" And what of it? Granted that, as a murderer, he deserved this punishment, what crime have you committed, poor fellow, that you should deserve to sit and see this show?

FIGURE 41

It should be stated here that Christians were killed in a myriad of ways. However, Christians were most often executed in the arena by means of one (or more) of the following punishments:

1. *ad bestias* or exposure to the beasts (e.g., *Martyrdom of Perpetua and Felicitas* 19–21)
2. *crematio* or execution by fire (e.g., *Martyrdom of Polycarp* 11–15)
3. *crucis supplicium* or crucifixion (e.g., Tacitus, *Annals* 15.44)

Numerous additional examples of all of these modes of execution can be gleaned from the stories of the martyrs. It should be also noted here that sometimes the penalties of *ad bestias* or *crematio* could be combined with crucifixion. For example, the female martyr Blandina was put on a cross and then exposed to a variety of wild beasts. Her death, along with the deaths of many other faithful Christians during the reign and with the full knowledge of the Emperor Marcus Aurelius (**see Figure 45**) is described in the *Letter of the Churches of Lyons and Vienne* (*Hist. eccl.* 5.1.41–42). Likewise, the martyr Poinius was nailed to a cross and then burned (*Martyrdom of Pionius the Presbyter and his Companions* 21).

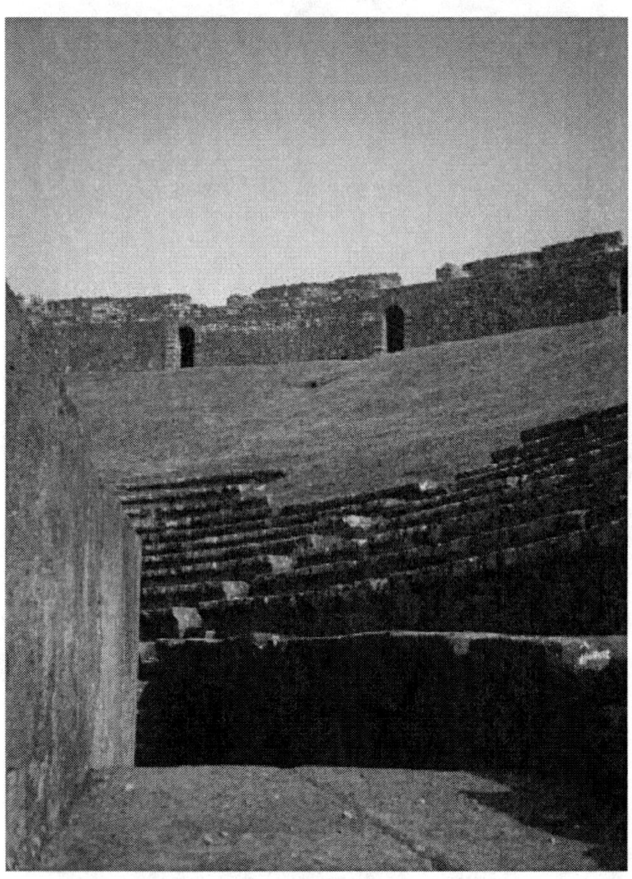

Figure 42

A particularly sick aspect of the Roman arena that was often related to the executions of Christians was the linkage of Greco-Roman mythological themes with the martyrs' deaths. In these deadly "plays," victims (whether Christian or not) were forced to don special costumes (e.g., *Martyrdom of Perpetua and Felicitas* 18) and play out the roles of various mythological heroes and heroines, with grim and bloody results (e.g., the battle of Hercules and the lion; the joining of King Minos daughter with the bull; Europa carried off by Zeus in the guise of a bull; see Martial, *On the Spectacles* 5, 7, 8, 21B and *1 Clement* 6.2).

Figure 43

After the noontime executions, the afternoon exhibition provided the real reason people came to the arena—the gladiatorial combats. Most gladiators were prisoners of war, slaves bought for the purpose, or criminals sentenced to serve in the gladiatorial schools. However, it was not uncommon for free people (usually, but not always, of low social standing) to sell themselves as gladiators because of the money to be made.

There were many types of gladiators who fought with different weapons and fighting styles. Probably the most recognizable of these to the modern mind is the *retarius* who was armed with a trident and a net to ensnare his opponent and protected only by a shoulder piece on their left side. This type of gladiator embodied the "fisherman." As such, it was only appropriate that these gladiators be matched against the heavily armed *myrmillo* or "fish-man" whose helmet had a fish-like crest. Other gladiator types included the *hoplomachus* who fought with a small round shield and carried a lance and short straight sword, the *Thracian* who carried a scimitar and a small square shield and the *essedarius* who fought from war chariots in the fashion of the British Celts.

FIGURE 44

Gladiators made up a peculiar and distinct class within Roman society. On the one hand, they were considered to be degraded people and social outcasts, being literally kept in chains when they were not training and fighting. On the other hand, gladiators had groups of devoted fans who admired them for their bravery, endurance and willingness to die. In addition, gladiators were viewed as ancient sex symbols. It was known that women, even those of high social standing, would pay a high price to spend the night with these men. Tertullian expresses this odd tension in public sentiment aptly:

> . . . those most loving gladiators, to whom men prostitute their souls, women too their bodies, slight and trample on them, though for their sakes they are guilty of the deeds they reprobate; nay, they doom them to ignominy and the loss of their rights as citizens, excluding them from the Curia, and the rostra, from senatorial and equestrian rank, and from all other honors as well as certain distinctions. What perversity! They have pleasure in those whom yet they punish; they put all slights on those to whom, at the same time, they award their approbation; they magnify the art and brand the artist. (*On the Spectacles* 22)

FIGURE 45

Further discussion of the arena lies outside the scope of this introduction. However, detailed descriptions of the gladiatorial events can be found in the bibliography that is provided.

Capitatis amputatio

The final form of punishment that we shall consider in this introduction is that of beheading. This type of execution was considered more humane because, if properly conducted, it was quick and relatively painless. Usually, this mode of death was reserved for citizens and the wealthy and elite of society. Although if we use the *Letter of the Churches of Lyons and Vienne* as a model, Roman citizenship did not guarantee a merciful death for every Christian (cf. the Roman citizen Attulus who was brutally killed in the amphitheatre [*Hist. eccl.* 5.1.44 and 52] and the other Christians who possessed citizenship who were beheaded [*Hist. eccl.* 5.1.47]). A number of famous Christians were executed in this manner including Paul (ca. 62; Acts of Paul 11.5), the famous Christian philosopher and apologist, Justin of Rome (ca. 165; *Martyrdom of the Holy Martyrs Justin, Chariton, Charito, Evelpistus, Hierax, Paeon and Liberian* 6) and Cyprian of Carthage (ca. 258; *Acts of Cyprian* 5).

PART 5
SOURCES FOR FURTHER STUDY: GETTING A "LAY OF THE LAND"

With these thoughts our introductory remarks reach their final phase. As is probably clear by now, the study of martyrdom and persecution in the early Church is a complex and multifaceted endeavor. By simply reading through this introduction you have, no doubt, realized that a veritable ocean of material for further study lies just under the surface. This is certainly the case yet this is no reason to be intimidated and as a result back away from this area of study. In this final section I will attempt to provide a brief outline of the major types of literature one comes in contact with when studying martyrdom and persecution in the early Church. Hopefully, this summary survey will help you navigate the sources referenced above and provide direction for locating other similar materials.

Four Categories of Literature

There are four primary categories of literature that one should be aware of as one proceeds to study martyrdom and persecution in the early Church: Non-Christian Testimonies, Apologies, Martyrologies, and Exhortations to Martyrdom. Each of these kinds of literature has something important to offer to one's understanding of the issues involved.

NON-CHRISTIAN TESTIMONIES

Non-Christian testimonies are extremely helpful in attempting to arrive at the fullest possible understanding of the conflict between Rome and the early Church. It must be understood from the outset that these sources are not friendly or sympathetic to Christianity. They are clearly biased. However, so are the Christian sources. For example, we moderns (influenced as we are by Christian documents) tend to think of the Roman officials as bloodthirsty "villains." Nevertheless when one reads Pliny's letter to Trajan it is clear that Pliny is really concerned about the potentially rebellious consequences of the Christian's "contumacious and inflexible obstinacy." Far from being desirous to see the Christians slaughtered, he clearly expresses his hope that many "might be reclaimed if a general pardon were granted to those who shall repent of their error." This implies that he has no personal vendetta against the Christians as individuals but rather fears the implications of what he sees as a politically questionable organization. Clearly, there is no such thing as an unbiased source so the best way we can get at the truth is to try to hear both sides of the argument. The non-Christian testimonies give the opportunity to attempt to do just this. Examples of this have been analyzed above such as Tacitus' report of the Neronic Persecution in *Annals* 15.44, Pliny's Letter to Trajan (*Ep.* 96) and Celsus' *On True Doctrine* (now found in fragmentary form in Origen's *Against Celsus*).

Apologies

Apology' comes from the Greek word 'apologia' which means "a speech in defense" and was used in legal settings for the defense offered by the accused in a judicial proceeding. A famous example of this is the apology offered by Socrates as he defended himself from the charge of corrupting the youth of Athens (see Plato, *Apology*).

Although the "apology" proper has legal roots, the early Christian apologies were not written for courtroom defense. Rather, they were attempts by early Christian thinkers to answer their critics. As Christianity developed, it faced criticism on two fronts: the Jewish community and the Greco-Roman world at large. This "two-front war" is captured by a statement of Paul concerning the overall reception of his preaching of Jesus' crucifixion: "For Jews demand signs and Greeks desire wisdom, but we proclaim Christ crucified, a stumbling block to Jews and foolishness to Gentiles, but to those who are the called, both Jews and Greeks, Christ the power of God and the wisdom of God" (1 Cor 1:22–24). Because the criticisms of these two communities were so different, early Christian apologetic literature took on completely divergent tones in order to respond to each group. On the one hand, Christians were forced to attempt to demonstrate to the Jewish community that their understanding of Jesus as "messiah" or, in Greek, "Christ" was the logical development of God's work with his chosen people and that the events of Jesus' life were, in fact, foretold by the Jewish prophets as part of God's plan to "redeem" Israel. On the other hand, Christians were called upon to refute the various charges brought against Christianity by the Greco-Roman world and show how Christian ideas were actually in harmony with the best ideas of Greco-Roman philosophy.

Apologetics aimed at Jewish Communities. The earliest communities of Jesus' followers were Jews. It is only logical to imagine that the very first people that they would have tried to convert to their way of thinking would have also been Jews. The New Testament is full of apologetic attempts on the part of various early Christian authors to "prove" the truth and/or superiority of Christian teaching by using the Scriptures (now known the Old Testament). In order to advance this agenda, the early Christians collected scriptural texts which scholars now call "testimonia." These texts were used to support key Christian teachings on the resurrection (e.g., Hos 6:1–2; cf. 1 Cor 15:4), Jesus' suffering and death (e.g., Isa 52–53; Ps 22; cf. 1 Cor 15:3 and Mark 15:34 respectively) and Jesus' origins (e.g., Isa 9:1–7; cf. Matt 4:14–16).

One of the most recognizable ways that Christians tried to convince other Jews of the truth of Christianity was by use of the "prophecy-fulfillment" motif found so readily in the Gospel of Matthew—captured in phrases such as "this was to fulfill what the prophet . . ." Other New Testament examples of Christian apologetics aimed at Judaism include: Stephen's speech in Acts 7, Paul's attempts to wrest the characters of Abraham and Sarah away from the Jews and make them examples for Christians of his day in Romans 4 and Galatians 4:21–31 and the book of Hebrews. Later examples of this type of literature include Justin's *Dialogue with Trypho* (ca. 155) and Tertullian's *Against the Jews* (ca. 200–206).

Apologetics aimed at the Greco-Roman World. More important for the purposes of studying martyrdom and persecution are the apologetic efforts directed against the Greco-Roman culture at large. The first full-scale apologies toward the Greco-Roman world appear in the second century. Among the most famous we can include, in Greek: Justin's *1 Apology* (ca. 150); Tatian's *Address to the Greeks* (ca. 170); Athenagoras' *Plea for the Christians* (ca. 177); Theophilus of Antioch's *To Autolycus* (ca. 180); Clement of Alexandria's *Exhortation to the Greeks* (ca. 180–200); Origen's *Against Celsus* (ca. 248) and in Latin: Tertullian's *Apology* (ca. 197) and *To Scapula* (ca. 212) and Minucius Felix's *Octavius* (ca. 218–235). This is not an exhaustive list. These apologies have as their goal the desire to protect the Church from popular violence and political oppression. In addition, the apologists hope to respond to the popular, political, and philosophical criticisms that were directed against the Church by the larger Greco-Roman society.

An important aspect of these apologies is the Christian defense mounted in an attempt to repulse the onslaught of Greco-Roman rumors and ill-informed accusations of atheism, sexual immorality, cannibalism and hatred of humanity which we discussed in detail above. Christians denied sexual excesses, pointing to the Christian bent toward chastity and sexual continence. Likewise, Christians refused to accept the charge that they failed to support the state, stating that they prayed for the welfare of both the Emperor and the Empire.

Far from limiting themselves to mere defense, early Christian apologists launched literary assaults on Greco-Roman religious beliefs and ritual practices, morality and philosophy. In making these counterattacks, the Christian apologists were actually revisiting the apologetic tradition of Hellenistic Judaism in which Jewish authors replied to many of the same accusations later leveled against the early Church. For example, the Christian apologists regularly attack the myths of the traditional Greco-Roman religions—such as that of Kronos eating his own children and Zeus' predilections for infidelity (cf. the Jewish philosopher, Philo, *The Decalogue* 53–55; *On the Contemplative Life* 6). For that matter, even Greco-Roman philosophers (Plato, *Euthyphro*) as well as writers (e.g., the Greek playwrights, Aeschylus and Euripides) and satirists (e.g., Lucian of Samosata) had ridiculed the cruder stories about the gods. Likewise, the apologists attack Greco-Roman idolatry and other expressions of worship. In this too they were merely restating older Jewish criticisms of the larger Greco-Roman culture (cf. Philo, *The Decalogue* 76–80; *On the Contemplative Life* 7–9).

Yet another topic of interest for the apologists is Greco-Roman philosophy but on this subject the apologists are divided. For example, apologists like Tatian, Theophilus and Athenagoras attack the philosophers as foolish and as those whose theories contradict each other. (Yet even in this they are not without precedent, cf. Lucian of Samosata, *Philosophies for Sale*.) Of a like mind is Tertullian, who expresses the extreme right-wing Christian position on Greco-Roman philosophy with his famous dictum: "What indeed has Athens to do with Jerusalem?" (*Prescription Against Heretics* 7.9). On the other side, writers like Justin and Clement of Alexandria do not wish to denigrate philosophy as a whole. Rather, they attribute the source of true philosophical wisdom to God. For example, according to Justin, each person's share of the truth is a result of the seeds of the Word (logos) that are present in all people. However, even with an enthusiast such as Justin this respect for philosophy is tempered by a sense that the truth was distorted (e.g., contradictions in various philosophical teachings) in its handing down (see Justin, *2 Apology* 10; cf. *2 Apology* 13).

Beyond these issues the apologists articulated Christian ideas on other, less popular Christian teachings such as creation *ex nihilo* ("out of nothing") and the resurrection. The idea of creation *ex nihilo* clashed with popular Greco-Roman philosophical teaching which envisioned God and matter as co-eternal. Likewise, Christian teaching on resurrection was perhaps the most difficult Christian doctrine for an educated Greco-Roman to accept.

Despite the myriad of issues the apologists do address it should be stressed here that they should not be read as if they present a complete picture of second or third century Christianity. They are keen to answer the objections of their critics but they spend little energy on issues such as the humanity and ministry of Jesus and the life and polity of the Church. Their scope is limited.

Martyrologies

A "martyrology" is a collection of stories of the martyrs. These stories are called either *martyrdoms* (or in Latin *passiones*) or *acts* (or in Latin *gesta*). In order to understand the role and purpose of these "martyrologies" one must first understand the Christian need for heroes and heroines as it faced the widespread opposition of the larger society. Initially, early Christians looked for inspiration in the heroic accounts of those non-Christians who died defending their faith in God. There are two key stories that influenced their ideas (and these were by no means the only ones): 1) the final days of Socrates as set forth in Plato's *Apology* (Socrates on trial for "corrupting the minds of the young" by challenging the traditional understanding of the gods) and *Phaedo* (Socrates' final words and execution) and 2) the Maccabean martyrs, particularly the stories of the aged Eleazar and the mother with her seven sons (see 2 Maccabees 6:18–7:41), who were faithful Jews who stood fast in defense of obedience to God's Torah.

A *martyrdom* is an account of the last days and death of a martyr or group of martyrs. The two earliest martyrdoms are the aforementioned *Martyrdom of Polycarp* (ca. 156) and the *Letter of the Churches of Vienne and Lyon* (ca. 177).

An *acts* is a recounting of the trial before the civil authorities of a martyr or group of martyrs. These are *not* simple transcripts of court proceedings. It should be remembered that while many of these acts are based of actual court documents, they have undergone Christian editing and adaptation. Some of the earliest examples of this kind of literature demonstrate this tendency to edit. For instance, the earliest example of this genre is the *Acts of Justin*. It exists in three variants that demonstrate the progressive editing that took place. The earliest example of this type of literature in Latin is the *Acts of the Scillitan Martyrs* (ca. 180) from North Africa. (Note: This is the earliest document from the North African Church.)

Exhortations to Martyrdom

An "exhortation to martyrdom" is a document written so as to encourage Christians facing persecution. Examples of this type of literature are Tertullian's *To the Martyrs* (ca. 197–203); Origen's *Exhortation to Martyrdom* (ca. 235) and Cyprian's *To Fortunatus* (ca. 257). The goals of this type of literature are manifest in the name of the literature itself.

A sample exhortation to martyrdom, in this case taken from the *Apocryphon of James* (Nag Hammadi Codex I, tract 2), will illustrate how such literature works better than any description (italics are mine):

> And I answered, and said to him: "Lord, we can obey you if you wish. For we have forsaken our forefathers and our mothers and our villages and have followed you. Grant us, therefore, not to be tempted by the wicked Devil." The Lord answered and said: "What is your merit when you do the will of the Father if it is given you by him as a gift, while you are tempted by Satan? But if you are oppressed by Satan and are persecuted and you do the Father's will, I say that he will love you and will make you equal with me and will consider that you have become beloved through his providence according to your free choice. Will you not cease, then, being lovers of the flesh and being afraid of sufferings? Or do you not know that you have not yet been mistreated and have not yet been accused unjustly, nor have you yet been shut up in prison, nor have you been condemned lawlessly, nor have you yet been crucified without reason, nor have you yet been buried shamefully, as was I myself, by the evil one? Do you dare to spare the flesh, you for whom the spirit is an encircling wall? *If you contemplate the world, how long is it before you—also how long it is after you, you will find that your life is a single day and your sufferings, one single hour.* For the good will not enter the world. Scorn death, therefore, and take concern for life. Remember my cross and my death and you will live."
>
> And I [James] answered and said to him: "Lord, do not mention to us the cross and the death, for they are far from you." The Lord answered and said: "Truly I say to you, none will be saved unless they believe in my cross. But those who have believed in my cross, theirs is the Kingdom of God. Therefore, become seekers of death, just as the dead who seek for life, for that which they seek is revealed to them. And what is there to concern them? When you turn yourselves towards death, it will make known to you

election. In truth I say to you, none of those who are afraid of death will be saved. For the Kingdom of God belongs to those who have put themselves to death. Become better than I; make yourselves like the son of the Holy Spirit!"

Other Available Sources

In delineating the above four main categories of literature, I do not mean to imply that the historian's sources are thereby exhausted. Certainly, there are other literary sources such as the *panegyric*, a eulogy or sermon delivered on the annual date commemorating a martyr's death. Many of these sermons were delivered by great bishops and preachers of the fourth and fifth centuries such as Basil of Caesarea, Gregory of Nazianzus, Gregory of Nyssa, John Chrysostom and Augustine of Hippo. The aim of these sermons was edification. Often their connection with history is *suspect*. In addition, there are sources such as the *Liber peristephanon* (*The Book of the Martyrs' Crowns*; compiled between 398–404) written by the Latin Christian poet, Prudentius. This work consists of fourteen hymns, each of which is devoted to a martyr, the vast majority of whom were either Spanish or Italian. For example, this is the key source for stories about the darkly comedic deacon, St. Laurence (d. 258) and the teenaged virgin, St. Agnes (d. 304). While these materials are not without value, they are of a clearly secondary character as regards history. Any student of martyrdom and persecution in the early Church is best served by focusing their attention on the four main categories outlined above.

Concluding Remarks

In the preceding pages I have attempted to introduce the subject of martyrdom and persecution in the early Church. My tactic has been to begin with a sketch of the beginnings of the conflict and how Jesus' execution as well as the language and teachings of Christianity set the stage for the violence that was to come. I moved on to consider the earliest clashes between the Christians and the various authorities of their geographical locations and chronological periods. With this we addressed some of the key criticisms leveled against the early Church by society at large. From these concepts we examined the Roman Imperial response and the tactics used against the early Church in an attempt to break its will. Lastly, we reviewed the various types of literature encountered by any student of this subject. It is my hope that this brief outline has been enlightening and that it will motivate further study.

Recommended Reading

Bowersock, Glen W., *Martyrdom and Rome* (Cambridge: Cambridge University Press, 1995).

- This is a brief discussion of martyrdom and persecution as faced by the Roman church.

Frend, W. H. C., *Martyrdom and Persecution in the Early Church* (Garden City, NY: Doubleday, 1967).

- The classic treatment of this topic in English. This work is a thorough examination of the major outbreaks of persecution based on a close analysis of the primary sources. The book is extremely long (over 700 pages) but well worth the time.

Mursurillo, Herbert, *The Acts of the Christian Martyrs* (Oxford: Clarendon, 1972).

- This is a one volume collection of many of the early martyrologies. It includes the original language and an English translation on opposite facing pages. Although the accuracy of the Greek or Latin manuscripts on which Mursurillo bases his translations has been questioned, the volume remains a standard.

A Basic Bibliography

Bauman, Richard A., *Crime and Punishment in Ancient Rome* (London: Routledge, 1996).

Clarke, G. W., trans., *The Octavius of Marcus Minucius Felix* (ACW 39; New York: Newman, 1974).

Crossan, John Dominic, "Bandit and Messiah," in idem., *The Historical Jesus: The Life of a Mediterranean Jewish Peasant* (San Francisco: Harper, 1991), 168–206.

Droge, Arthur J. and James D. Tabor, *A Noble Death: Suicide and Martyrdom Among Christians and Jews in Antiquity* (San Francisco: Harper, 1992).

Foerster, Werner, "κύριος," *TDNT* 3.1039–58.

Gamble, Harry Y., "Apologetics," in Everett Ferguson, ed., *Encyclopedia of Early Christianity* (2nd ed.; 2 vols.; New York: Garland, 1997), 2.81–87.

Grant, Michael, *Gladiators* (London: Weidenfeld & Nicolson, 1967)—reprint, New York: Barnes and Noble, 1995.

Grant, Robert M., *Greek Apologists of the Second Century* (Philadelphia: Westminster, 1988).

Isaac, Benjamin, "Banditry," *ABD* 1.575–80.

Kyle, Donald G., *Spectacles of Death in Ancient Rome* (London: Routledge, 1998).

Molinari, Andrea Lorenzo, *Climbing the Dragon's Ladder: The Martyrdom of Perpetua and Felicitas* (Eugene, Ore.: Wipf and Stock, 2006).

O'Collins, Gerald G., "Crucifixion," *ABD* 1.1207–10.

Preisker, Herbert, "κλέπτω, κλέπτῃ," *TDNT* 3.754–56.

Radice, Betty, trans., *Pliny: Letters, Books VIII-X, Panegyricus* (LCL 59; Cambridge, Mass.: Harvard University Press, 1969).

Rapske, Brian, *Paul in Roman Custody* (The Book of Acts in its First Century Setting 3; Grand Rapids, Mich.: Eerdmans, 1994).

Rengstorf, Karl H., "λῃστής," *TDNT* 4.257–62.

Rhee, Helen, *Early Christian Literature: Christ and Culture in the Second and Third Centuries* (Early Church Monographs; London: Routledge, 2005).

Salisbury, Joyce E., *Perpetua's Passion: The Death and Memory of a Young Roman Woman* (London: Routledge, 1997).

________, *The Blood of Martyrs: Unintended Consequences of Ancient Violence* (London: Routledge, 2004).

Schneemelcher, Wilhelm, ed., *New Testament Apocrypha, Volume 2: Writings Related to the Apostles; Apocalypses and Related Writings* (rev. ed.; Louisville: Westminster/ Knox, 1992).

Sordi, Marta, *The Christians and the Roman Empire* (Norman, Okla.: University of Oklahoma Press, 1986).

Stark, Rodney, *The Rise of Christianity: A Sociologist Reconsiders History* (Princeton, N.J.: Princeton University Press, 1996).

Wiedemann, Thomas, *Emperors and Gladiators* (London: Routledge, 1992).

Wilken, Robert L., *The Christians as the Romans Saw Them* (New Haven, Conn.: Yale University Press, 1984).

Figure Captions

Figure 1

This scene is taken from the Gospel of Matthew 14:28–33. Matthew, dependent on the Gospel of Mark 6:45–52 as a primary source retells the story of Jesus Walking on the Water. However, Matthew adds the material found in 14:28–33. In this variant, when Jesus identifies himself to his disciples who are in the boat, Peter asks permission to walk out on the water to meet Jesus. Jesus consents to Peter's request and Peter gets out of the boat and comes to Jesus. However, Peter becomes distracted by the wind and begins to sink crying, "Lord, save me!" Jesus immediately grabs Peter's hand and chides him for his "little faith." Yet, Peter was the only one with enough faith to come to Jesus. This Petrine tradition is unique to Matthew.

Figure 2

This is a scene taken from the Gospel of John 18:10–12. This story of an altercation during Jesus' arrest in which a disciple attacks one of Jesus' assailants and cuts off his ear is common to all four canonical gospels. However, only John identifies Peter as the one who perpetrates this assault. Later, the great Carthaginian theologian, Tertullian (late 2nd to early 3rd century AD) would write in support of Christian pacifism, "But how will a Christian man war, no, how will he serve even in peace, without a sword, which the Lord has taken away? For albeit soldiers had come unto John, and had received the formula of their rule; albeit, likewise, a centurion had believed; still the Lord afterward, in disarming Peter, unbelted every soldier" (*On Idolatry* 19).

Figure 3

Simon Magus, Peter's "arch enemy" in the *Acts of Peter*, falls from the sky. This scene from *Acts of Peter* 31–32 depicts the climactic moment in the clash between Peter and Simon. As a final attempt to gain religious ascendancy over Peter, Simon vows to demonstrate his superiority by flying over Rome and returning to God "whose power I am, although enfeebled." For a moment Simon is successful in his promise of achieving flight but is brought crashing back down to earth at the prayer of Peter. Careful to present Peter as merciful, the narrator describes Peter's prayer as specifically requesting that Simon not die as a result of his descent but, rather, that he merely "break his leg in three places." Sure enough, Simon is injured in exactly this way. Shortly after, he dies at the hands of a surgeon.

Figure 4

This scene depicts the *Domine, quo vadis*? story. The legend, recorded in *Acts of Peter* 35, describes the situation in which Peter, leaving Rome in disguise because of persecution, encounters Jesus on the *Via Appia*, headed into Rome to be "crucified again." See the full discussion of this legend in the Preface of this volume.

Figure 5

This picture, along with the following three, displays a section from the famous bronze door through which one can enter into St. Peter's Basilica in Rome. This door, which was commissioned by Pope Eugene IV, was completed in 1455 by Antonio Averulino, also known as Il Filarete. In its entirety it is comprised of six panels. The top two depict Jesus and Mary enthroned. The first of the middle two panels displays Paul with the sword, symbolic of both his theological use of God's word and the instrument of his death. The second of the two middle panels is a rendering of Peter giving the keys, symbolic of ecclesiastical authority, to the kneeling Pope Eugene IV. Finally, the two lowest panels are representations of the martyrdoms of Peter and Paul.

The Martyrdom of Peter, positioned in the lower right corner of the door, shows Peter being led away from a seated Roman official. One presumes that this is Nero, although in the *Acts of Peter* it is not Nero but the Roman Prefect Agrippa who sentences Peter to death. The procession winds around toward the upper left portion of the piece and finally ends in a depiction of Peter being crucified upside down.

Figure 6

Detail of Peter's crucifixion. Two executioners stand on parallel ladders that have been positioned so as to facilitate his feet being nailed to the cross. Below, two others drive nails into Peter's hands. The *Acts of Peter* has Peter explain the symbolism behind the positioning utilized in his execution as evocative of the grievous situation of the first man and all of humanity who, along with Adam, is "falling head-downwards" and in need of the Savior. Conversely, many Christians would claim that the reason for Peter's head downward positioning is because he requested it saying, ". . . I am not worthy to be crucified like my Lord." This tradition comes to us through the *Acts of Peter and Paul* (a.k.a. *Ps.-Marcellus*).

Figure 7

This panel of the Martyrdom of Paul is more complex than that of the Martyrdom of Peter. It is located on the lower left section of the door. When it is viewed from left to right, it portrays Paul being led away after having been sentenced by Nero. On the lower right side it shows the moment immediately before the actual martyrdom of Paul, in which Paul kneels blindfolded before his executioner.

A final point of interest is found in the top middle portion of the composition in which Paul is depicted reaching through the clouds, as if from Heaven. The recently executed Paul is shown handing a blindfold to a woman who kneels beneath him. The woman is Plautilla, known to us from the Latin *Passion of Paul* (a.k.a. *Ps.-Linus*). According to this legend, Paul meets Plautilla, a noble matron, while being led away to his execution. He borrows a handkerchief from her so as to blindfold his eyes and tells the woman that she must wait for him and, after his death; he will return it to her. Paul is then led away. When the soldiers return from their grim work, they encounter Plautilla who is rejoicing. Thinking that she is crazy, they taunt her. In response, she shows them the very blindfold she had given Paul, stained with the saint's blood. To their utter amazement, she explains that Paul, along with a celestial company, appeared to her and returned the handkerchief.

Figures 8a and 8b

Detail of Paul's execution.

Figure 9

This is the altar of Saints Processus and Martinianus from St. Peter's Basilica. It is the main altar located in the north transept. Behind the altar one can see the mosaic of the martyrdom of Processus and Martinianus which was completed by Fabio Cristofari in 1737 from the original oil painting by Jean 'Valentin' de Boulogne, now in the Vatican Pinacoteca.

Figure 10

The Martyrdom of St. Processus and St. Martiniano, a 17th century oil painting by Jean 'Valentin' de Boulogne. This painting actually depicts the torture of the two saints, as according to legend, they were beheaded. The two men are stretched out on a rack with three torturers engaged in their abuse. One strains against the rack, attempting to stretch the men's bodies out still further. Another kneels, heating up an iron poker in the smoldering coals of a fire. The third, his back turned to the viewer, prepares to unleash a blow with his rod. Above the martyrs an angel descends, holding out the palm branch of martyrdom.

Figure 11

This poignant sign is posted just inside the entrance to the Mammertine Prison in Rome as a grim reminder of those who testified to their faith, enduring incarceration. In addition to Peter and Paul and their converts, Processus and Martinianus, others listed include Pope Sixtus II and the famous Deacon Lawrence. Both men died during the Valerian Persecution of AD 257–60. If one looks closely, one will note that this sign wrongly situates their deaths during the Decian Persecution (AD 249–251).

Figures 12–13

This altar is located in the bowels of the Mammertine Prison in Rome. It was here that Peter and Paul were reputed to have been held as they awaited their executions. The altar commemorates their captivity and their conversion of their jailors, Processus and Martinianus, and some forty-seven other prisoners who shared their fate.

Figure 14

This is the marble plaque that is located to the left of the Mammertine altar commemorating the conversion of Processus and Martinianus. It reads, "Questa é la colonna dove stando legati i SS. Apostoli Pietro e Paolo convertirno i SS. Martiri Processo e Martiniano custodi delle carceri et altri XLVII alla fede di Cristo quali battezzorno coll'acqua di questo fonte scaturita miracolosamente" (This is the column to which Saints Peter and Paul, being tied up, converted to the Christian Faith the holy martyrs Processus and Martinianus [jailers] and another forty-seven people, who were all baptized with the water of this spring, miraculously come to life.).

Figure 15

The Crucifixion of St. Peter (1600) by Michelangelo Merisi da Carvaggio, located in the Cerasi Chapel inside Santa Maria del Popolo, Rome.

Figure 16

This powerful painting of the crucifixion of St. Peter is located to the right of the altar in the Church of Domine, Quo Vadis?

Figure 17

The old gate on the *Via Appia*. Legend says that Peter passed through this gate on his way out of Rome.

Figures 18–19

The Church Santa Maria in Palmis, better known as the Church of Domine, Quo Vadis?, is situated about 800m from the St. Sebastian Gate or Porta San Sebastiano outside the Aurelian Walls south of Rome on the *Via Appia*, where the *Via Ardeatina* branches off the Via *Appia*.

Figure 20

According to legend, the two footprints on a marble slab at the center of the Church of Domine, Quo Vadis? are supposed to be those of Jesus himself, left behind as miraculous sign. (The original marble slab is found in the nearby Basilica of San Sebastiano.)

Figure 21

This is the denial of Christ by Peter, part of the Holy Door by Vico Consorti (1949) which leads into St. Peter's Basilica in Rome.

Figure 22

It should never be forgotten that crucifixion was a terrible death. A victim was stretched out and left hanging, suspended between heaven and earth, damned to gasp out slowly their last breaths in appalling pain. This crucifix can be found in San Damiano, the church made famous by St. Francis of Assisi (Assisi, Italy).

Figure 23

According to the placard over Jesus' head (Mark 15:26 and par./ John 19:19–20), he was executed because he posed a political threat to the Romans. Both Mark and Matthew claim that Jesus was crucified with others associated with political rebellion. This panel, one of sixteen, is part of the Holy Door by Vico Consorti (1949) which leads into St. Peter's Basilica in Rome.

Figure 24

Nero Claudius Drusus Germanicus was emperor of Rome from AD 54–68. Nero's life reads like a soap opera (see the accounts of Tacitus and Suetonius) but for our purposes, it is his city-wide persecution of Christians in the wake of the Great Fire of Rome in AD 64 that lends his name infamy.

Figure 25

These are reputed to be the chains that were used to restrain Peter. As the story goes, there were originally two sets of chains, one length that bound Peter in Jerusalem, the other while he was in Rome. A thirteenth century legend claims that a miracle joined the two chains. They are housed in the Church of San Pietro in Vincoli (St. Peter in Chains), which is located just a short distance north of the Coliseum.

FIGURE 26

This statue of Paul is situated in the middle of a quadriportico which ushers the visitor into the church of St. Paul Outside the Walls. Originally, a small shrine was built over the spot where St. Paul himself was allegedly buried. In the fourth century, the Emperor Constantine built a large basilica over the older structure. Sadly, this amazing basilica was destroyed by a fire in 1823. It was rebuilt over the same foundations.

FIGURE 27

This famous statue of St. Peter is located in St. Peter's Square, to the left of the main door of the Basilica as one ascends the steps. It was carved by Guiseppe de Fabris in 1838–1840. Originally, it had been commissioned by Pope Gregory XVI (1831–1846) for St. Paul Outside the Walls. It was moved to St. Peter's Square in 1947 by Pope Pius IX.

The location for this statue is poignant and deserves some explanation. In the middle of the first century AD, Nero's grandmother, Agrippina senior, drained the Vatican Hill and constructed terraced gardens on this site and even a covered path to the Tiber. When Nero inherited the gardens after murdering his mother in AD 59, these gardens were flourishing. He built a bridge over the Tiber so that whenever he wished he could enjoy his gardens or visit the circus which his predecessor Caligula had made on the lower ground. These gardens and the nearby circus were Nero's favorite places. Nero loved to drive his chariots and enjoyed the obligatory cheers of his embarrassed subjects.

We are told by the Roman historian Tacitus (*Annals* 15.44) that, during the time of the Neronic Persecution, that Nero offered his gardens and the circus as the venue for these executions. Thus it was on the Vatican Hill itself where Nero organized his spectacles of carnage and brutality at the expense of the Christians. It is therefore possible that Peter may have met his death on this very site.

FIGURE 28

Mars, the god of war (Capitoline Museum, Rome).

FIGURE 29

Diana, the goddess of the hunt (Capitoline Museum, Rome).

FIGURE 30

Minerva, goddess of wisdom (Capitoline Museum, Rome).

FIGURE 31

Venus, the goddess of love (Capitoline Museum, Rome).

FIGURE 32

Mercury, the messenger of the gods (Capitoline Museum, Rome).

FIGURE 33

Marcus Ulpius Traianus was emperor of Rome from AD 98–117. He is particularly significant in any study of martyrdom and persecution in earliest Christianity because of an exchange of letters between himself and Pliny the Younger, governor of Bithynia. Their correspondence represents the first extant Roman discussion of the 'Christian problem' and how to deal with this perceived threat from a legal standpoint.

Figure 34

Gaius Messius Quintus Trajanus Decius was emperor of Rome from AD 249–251. He was one of a string of 'soldier emperors' that rose to power through violence in the third century. Upon his accession to the throne, Decius sought to unify the Empire by requiring that everyone offer sacrifice to the traditional gods. The results were absolutely devastating to the Christian communities. Sometimes it is asserted that it was under his reign that the Church experienced its first world-wide (i.e., Empire-wide persecution) persecution. This is only true in that Christians were martyred for their faith all over the Empire. However, this does *not* mean that Decius targeted Christians. The extant evidence, namely certificates of sacrifice that have survived, indicate that his requirement of sacrifice was a uniform demand and did not single out Christians.

Figure 35

Lucius Septimius Severus Pertinax was emperor of Rome from AD 193–211. It was during his reign that the famous Carthaginian saints Perpetua and Felicitas were killed. (Perpetua is the first known woman Christian writer by virtue of her extant diary which is part of the *Martyrdom of Perpetua and Felicitas*.) In addition, it was also about this time that Leonides, the father of the famous biblical theologian Origen, was martyred in Alexandria. It is suggested by some that Septimius Severus promulgated an edict against the Christians which resulted in these sporadic persecutions but evidence is scanty.

Figure 36

This is the ancient opening through which prisoners were lowered into the bowels of the Mammertine Prison, a subterranean holding area.

Figures 37–40

The Roman Coliseum is also known as the Flavian amphitheater as a credit to the emperors who were responsible for its construction. It was begun in AD 72 under the Emperor Vespasian and completed during the reign of his son, Titus in 80. It was constructed over the remains of Nero's "Golden House" in Rome. The primary function of this, as with any, amphitheater was to house spectacles of blood sports (Latin *munera*), i.e., wild beast hunts and combats (morning events), execution of criminals (midday intermission events), and gladiatorial combats which sometimes included mock sea battles (afternoon events). A number of early Christians lost their lives in this building, although, contrary to popular conception, this building was not in existence during the Neronic Persecution.

The design of an amphitheater basically requires the construction of two semicircular theaters placed face to face. Within this design, tiers of seats are supported by vaulted substructures that allow easy access into the seating area. The arena floor hides an extremely complex system of animal pens and storage rooms. In addition, a series of passages through these areas allow for the arena staff to move animals, gladiators, prisoners, scenery and other equipment. Elevators raised and lowered animals, people and objects to the floor of the arena from the areas below. The seating capacity of the Coliseum is estimated around 50,000.

FIGURES 41-42

This is the amphitheater in Pompeii. It was destroyed in the eruption of Mount Vesuvius along with the rest of the city on August 24, AD 79. Although some anti-Christian graffiti has been found in Pompeii, there is no evidence that any Christians lost their lives in this building. It is merely one example of many amphitheaters just like it that were sprinkled throughout the Roman Empire. For example, a small Roman amphitheater exists, albeit in a ruined state, not far outside of Assisi, Italy. Its existence in a relatively small city like Pompeii serves as a reminder of the threat faced by all Christians, not just those who lived in metropolitan centers such as Alexandria, Carthage, Rome and Antioch.

FIGURES 43–44

This is all that is left of the amphitheater in Carthage, Africa Proconsularis. Many scholars believe that it was here that Perpetua and Felicitas and their companions met their deaths on March 7, 203. Now all that remains of the building, believed to be second only to the Coliseum in seating capacity, is the wall that separated the "box seats" of the wealthy and affluent from the carnage taking place on the arena floor. Today, a small shrine to Perpetua and Felicitas is built into the middle of the amphitheater.

FIGURE 45

Marcus Aurelius Antoninus was emperor of Rome from AD 161–180. He has come to be known as a philosopher-king because of his adherence to Stoic philosophy as is demonstrated in his famous literary work, *Meditations*. However, it is clear that during his reign the relative clemency of the legislation of Trajan was replaced with a harsher tone. There is ample literary evidence that demonstrates the anti-Christian climate during his reign. Among these texts are the acts of Justin and his companions who suffered at Rome (ca. 165), of Carpus, Papylus, and Agathonica, who were martyred in Asia Minor, the Scillitan Martyrs in Numidia, and the touching Letters of the Churches of Lyons and Vienne (Eusebius, *Hist. eccl.*, 5.1–4) in which is contained the description of the tortures inflicted (177) on Blandina and her companions at Lyons. This document throws light on the character and extent of the persecution of the Christians in southern Gaul, and the role of the emperor therein.